ETHICS PROBLEM SOLVING AND DISCOURSE ON LIVING

Murray I. Mantell

University Press of America,® Inc.
Lanham · Boulder · New York · Toronto · Plymouth, UK

Copyright © 2011 by
University Press of America,® Inc.
4501 Forbes Boulevard
Suite 200
Lanham, Maryland 20706
UPA Acquisitions Department (301) 459-3366

Estover Road
Plymouth PL6 7PY
United Kingdom

All rights reserved
Printed in the United States of America
British Library Cataloging in Publication Information Available

Library of Congress Control Number: 2010943264
ISBN: 978-0-7618-5416-6 (paperback : alk. paper)
eISBN: 978-0-7618-5417-3

∞™ The paper used in this publication meets the minimum requirements of American National Standard for Information Sciences—Permanence of Paper for Printed Library Materials, ANSI Z39.48-1992

Contents

Preface		v
Introduction		vii
1	Origins of Ethics	1
2	Approaches to Ethical Behavior	5
3	Definitions and Basic Assumptions	11
4	Principles and Rules	15
5	Problem Solving Procedure	17
6	Definitions and Essays	23

Preface

This text is written with the goal of providing assistance in the teaching of ethics at all levels from grade school to the practicing professional; and for individuals seeking self-help material for guidance in living. The text begins with a discussion of the origins of ethics and of the common (faulty) approaches to ethical behavior. The determination of right or wrong is always dependent on clearly understood and agreed upon basic assumptions. The ontological arguments and logic used to establish these necessary basic assumptions are presented in Chapter 3. The resulting culmination is a simple practical procedure, based on Kant's Categorical Imperative (the Universal Law), which can permit everyone to determine for themselves right or wrong or what ought to be done in any situation.

Real communication depends on agreement upon the meaning of the words used in communication. Ordinary dictionaries, such as Webster's, in providing meaning of words often provide multiple meanings for the same word. In ordinary discourse, all too often a listener may assume a particular one of the multiple meanings of a word is being used, while the speaker is using a different one of the multiple meanings of the word; thus, there is no real communication. Chapter 6 attempts to provide an integrated set of definitions with a single unambiguous meaning for each word, which when used in ethical discourse, has the potential to significantly improve the level of success that can be achieved in solving problems, resolving conflicts non-violently, and accomplishing goals. Many of these definitions are adaptations from the "Ethics" of Benedict De Spinoza who probably has done the most comprehensive work of presenting a studied integrated set of definitions of the intangibles.

Most of the words needed for ethical discourse can be adequately defined with a single phrase or sentence. However, many complex concepts such as truth, good, justice, etc. require supplemental essays to clearly understand the meaning of the word, so that it may be used effectively in ethical discourse. Chapter 6 also includes some 50 essays related to specific definitions which were deemed to need clarification. These essays alone can provide a base for thoughtful ethical discourse along a wide range of subject matter.

Introduction

Most people's daily lives center on the problems of mere existence. They must work today so that they may earn money to buy food, clothing and shelter; so that they will be able to work tomorrow, so that they may earn money to be able to be able to work the next day to earn money, to..., ad infinitum. The struggle for mere physical existence has been so severe, and still is for many, that there has been little time for thinking of anything beyond the problems of survival. However, now that science and engineering have opened the way for easing the burden of survival, there is time for many more to reflect on what there is beyond mere existence-on what is the purpose of man's existence. The general public all too often is concerned with what exists or what happens and neglect completely what matters. The consideration of what matters, of what ought to be done, or the study of values and duty in human conduct, is the field of ethics.

Life continuously forces us to make decisions--to choose between right and wrong, to approve or disapprove. A life which is concerned primarily with mere physical existence or material comfort, without other goals or a sense of direction, tends to react by impulse, force of habit, inertia, or the flip of a coin; and when leisure comes, we hear the continual cry of the unguided: "Let's do something," "Let's go somewhere." We must assume that one form of conduct may be more likely to accomplish one's purpose better than another. Ethics should show direction and the scale of values to choose those forms of conduct which tend to fulfill these purposes.

Chapter One

Origins of Ethics

Primitive man's struggles for existence necessitated certain actions which would be considered ethical in character. Hunger and thirst and the need for protection against "cold, wind and rain" were amongst the stimuli which developed the desirable attributes of industriousness and prudence. The hostility of animals and of other men demanded of those who survived that temper be replaced by self control, gluttony and drunkenness by temperance, carelessness by competence, indifference by concern, etc.

Devotion to mate, children, family, and the advantages offered by cooperation of a close group or tribe brought about the need for development of customs or unwritten laws of proper conduct for all the member of the social group. Those tribes that developed the ability to work together had a marked advantage in their capability to both provide and protect. Thus, social characteristics such as loyalty, obedience and mutual service tended to replace greed, lust, caprice and internal quarreling. Actions by one individual which were disagreeable to the tribe were readily evident in the close daily relations that existed. The non-conformist very quickly became aware of the resentment, anger, contempt, ridicule, or rebuke of the tribe. Conversely, actions considered proper and desirable were responded to promptly by praise and honor. The individual had to conform or to be ready to undergo the severe additional hazards of living alone.

As tribal groups merged to form nations, they usually found that individual and different tribal customs were not satisfactory for the harmony of the entire group. Hence, the ruling authority of the nation often found it desirable and necessary to establish a uniform written code which supplanted various unwritten customs of the separate tribes (e.g., the code of Hammurabi in Babylonia, the code of Deuteronomy including the Ten Commandments, and the Code of Manu of the Hindus which amongst its detailed commandments over daily living, fixed the caste system of India). Whereas many of the customs and codes were initiated with foresight and wisdom, other ruling authorities imposed generally abhorrent customs such as caste, dueling, slavery, human sacrifice, cannibalism, infanticide, and senicide (killing the elderly at a fixed age). Undoubtedly, in most of these instances, there was no valid standard of judgment or continuous reflective thought to evaluate existing customs when a custom needed changing or to determine if a new custom was better than the old. Customs and codes were followed by the more comprehensive legal systems of common law and statutes representing more or less the minimum ethics which the majority of the people would accept. Here again, the legal systems require a standard of judgment to evaluate where the law represents special privilege, obsolete application, or poor adjudication.

As the social community increased in size, the danger from animals decreased, the struggle for existence softened, and many of the stimuli for ethical progress tended to be removed. In the crowded community, it is much easier to live a life which is relatively isolated from the scrutiny of others. The criminal can hide much more easily in the crowded city than was possible in the narrow confines of the tribal community. In the large community, it becomes more difficult to know who is responsible for shoddy goods and many other kinds of unethical action may tend to flourish undetected. Whereas primitive man worked off his energies and thus quieted his impulses and passions, the relatively monotonous occupations of the city dweller creates restlessness and a craving for excitement which tends to breed delinquency and criminal activities.

With increasing civilization, some aid to ethical progress came about through the development of that which we call conscience. Certain actions are followed by pleasure; others by pain and disaster. These experiences and the accumulated knowledge of customs, codes, and statutes are the base from which conscience develops. Conscience can be particularly valuable in an emergency, when there is no time for reflection. But just as our total memory of long past happenings is bound to be subject to error frequently, so may the part of our memory related to proper actions (conscience) be subject to frequent error. Conscience differs widely with the experiences of the individual and his reactions to his unique environment, and if the environment, customs and codes are wrong, then the base from which the conscience develops is wrong.

Evolutionary natural selection, custom, codes, conscience, and legal systems all have made contributions to ethical progress; however, even our highly complex modern legal system dictates proper conduct for only a small percentage of the innumerable daily actions of the individual, and all of the above factors are subject to considerable error in their applications. The major advance in ethical progress came with the development of formalized comprehensive reflective ethical theories which were potentially applicable to every action of every individual.

Chapter Two

Approaches to Ethical Behavior

Every person probably has at least some vague, superficial, unorganized ideas about the difference between right and wrong, the meaning of life, happiness, success, beauty, and many other concepts involved in everyday affairs. We continuously receive these ideas from family and friends and from home, school, and religious institutions. The following examples outline some commonly stated general approaches to ethical behavior and an evaluation of a few of the complex problems one faces in using each of these individual approaches.

Obey the laws of the land. The law is often indicated to be the minimum ethics which a particular society will accept. However, does the individual have the responsibility to judge the merit of the laws, or merely to obey? Our present legal system appears to be a confused mixture of acting as a threat to potential criminals, a device for removal from society, a ritual of expiation, and a prompter for moral reform. General attitudes of avoiding individual responsibility, of "let the government do it," have resulted in hundreds upon hundreds of legislators at all levels of government, diligently and continuously writing thousands upon thousands of laws. The legislators, in their anxiety to cover all actions, have often brought forth amateurish, excessive, inapplicable, and unenforceable laws. For example, laws have been passed which prohibit (a) walking through the streets with shoelaces undone, (b) wearing of suspenders, (c) biting one's landlord, (d) dogs from crying, (e) tickling a girl, (f) a woman from buying a new hat without her husband trying it on first, (g) riding on the roof of a taxicab, and (h) a housewife from moving the furniture in her home without her husband's consent. Laws tend to emphasize the negative, pointing out what is considered wrong but rarely point out what is considered right. It is much easier to write new laws than it is to make the new law effective. It is fairly safe to say that few people obey all laws, particularly the many obsolete laws which have not been repealed. The mere passing of a law does not necessarily make people ethical. Even the lawyers, in their professional activities, have an extra-legal province of professional ethics. There are laws of right which are higher than the laws of the land. We must seek this higher standard to judge whether new laws are needed, whether a law is obsolete, whether a law is good, and to allow each individual deliberate, reasoned choice of action.

Follow the recognized customs and ideals. This may be considered a more comprehensive approach than merely following the laws, as one part of the customs of a society. However, customs and ideals as well as laws, may not be rational in origin; often, they are imposed by an individual or group in a position to dominate lives. Even if the custom and ideals were originally rational in origin, this approach implies that we must forever hold to them blindly or all is lost. Customs of the past have included cannibalism, incest, witch burning, and slavery. When a custom is in force, the path of least resistance is to conform, but can we afford to conform at the expense of truth, reason, and justice? We cannot be content to know what the customs and ideals are and merely follow; but we must ask what they ought to be.

Follow the example of great men. We may well follow the example of Christ, Buddha or Gandhi. However, many have followed the examples of Hitler and Mussolini. The major obstacles in this approach are the difficulty of knowing enough about any man's life to be able to have examples to follow for each of life's many problems and, most important, to have a standard by which to judge what man is truly great and deserves to be followed.

Follow the "Good Book" and religious authority. Many people do profess to follow a religion; many others are ignorant of and do not follow the religion to which they profess. When the "Good Book" is spoken of, some speak of the New Testament; others speak of the Old Testament, and still others speak of the Book of Mormon, the Koran, the Bhagavad Gita, the Tao Te Ching, or the Analects of Confucius. Does a Buddhist or a member of any other of the hundreds of different religious sects, have good reason to follow the religion in which he was born and brought up, without fully considering all of the other religions? Assuming the particular "Good Book" and religion have been chosen wisely, can we be sure that the religious authorities are interpreting the ideals correctly? Religious authorities have built great organizations to aid in extending ideals, but too often the ideals have been forgotten and attention centered in the organization. Yet someone must interpret the will of God, at least about such modern innovations as television, nuclear energy, and space travel which do not appear to be mentioned as such in the "Good Books." Historically, it can be seen that the will of God has been interpreted to justify such actions as animal and human sacrifice, burning at the stake and massacres of the unbelievers. Most people would justify promoting the commandment. "Thou shalt not kill" by taking the weapon of a potential murderer, without his knowledge and thus breaking the commandment "Thou shalt not steal." Similarly, even the very devout would justify working on the Sabbath if otherwise the safety of an entire community would be in jeopardy. The faithful practice of a religion is a very complex and difficult task. There are probably no ethical situations which are exactly the same as those found in religious precedent. Apparently, some other outside means or standard is needed to determine if religious ideals are being interpreted and applied correctly, and upon occasion to justify breaking of the ideal.

Strive for the welfare of society. No man can live adequately alone. Men are largely affected by circumstances, and therefore many have made one of their great aims in life the improvement of man's external conditions--his society. Indeed, throughout history there have been numerous individuals and nations who considered themselves the ones most capable of leading other individuals and nations in the direction of the ideal society; those who disagreed were often put to the sword. Do we want the regimentation of the totalitarian state which may decide that individuals must be sacrificed for the good of the state? How does one know what is good for the state? It is too easy for the state to do something wrong if it doesn't have to take the time to make the one who is sacrificing believe and want to do so voluntarily. Society and the state are made possible by some subordination of the individual, and the individual ordinarily gains more than he loses by subordination; however, the subordination should be voluntary, for the state exists for the individual, not the individual for the state. If the individual must yield before force, the decision has no ethical value for him. If we strive for the welfare of a state which leaves men free to reason and to act, a state which places in the most honorable and commanding position the intellectually and ethically elite, again we must first accomplish a most complex and difficult outside task to establish and interpret the ideals upon which it must be founded. For example, communism expresses the ideal: "From everyone according to his abilities, and to everyone according to his needs;" but how is one to determine who "needs" an automobile or a television set when there are not enough for all? Desiring to strive for the welfare of society, but not knowing what kind of a society one should strive for, is like desiring to aid the sick but through ignorance giving poison instead of medicine.

Follow one's conscience. What we consider right or wrong is largely dependent upon what one is used to, becoming in essence, conditioned reflexes which may be called the conscience. The conscience may be a prior judgment of right and wrong, and anticipation of the opinions of others, or fear of punishment. It develops from prior experiences with the laws, customs, ideals, religion, and the totality of society and the environment. As each new situation is at least slightly different from those prior, it is relatively easy to rationalize away the conscience. It could be said that the conscience causes a man to follow, as a man follows the automobile he drives. The conscience tends to be primarily negative in determining what is wrong, but not what is right. We hear and speak of people who have no conscience; but, more correctly, it should be said that their conscience is different. It is to be expected that if the past environment is different and wrong, then the conscience may develop to be different and wrong. Thus, each man needs some outside standard by means of which he can check the fallibility of his conscience.

Follow reason and logic. It has been said that if one wishes to be the monarch of a little world, command thyself through reason, but all too few can reason well or desire to reason. Too many men reason primarily about what they have done, instead of what they should do. Much of each man's world is there by precedent, and it is difficult to reason him out of something he was never reasoned into. Reason and the logic of the syllogism are closely allied. A syllogism may have a major premise, a minor premise and a conclusion, respectively such as all ducks have web feet. Donald is a duck; therefore, Donald has web feet. However, Donald may have no feet; a "logical" conclusion has been obtained, but it is based upon the incorrect major premise that all ducks have web feet. Thus, reason cannot stand by itself; there must at least be truths to reason with. Also, mere reason cannot determine its own insufficiency and the difference between right and wrong reasoning; nor can it judge the quality of reasoning, for some reasoning must be better than others. One can no more follow reason alone, than the eye alone seeing something exists can judge whether or not it should exist.

Strive for happiness. Of all the millions who are frenziedly seeking happiness, all too few know just what they are seeking. Some think of happiness as being wealth, power, fame, or sensual pleasure. Wealth can be a burden that only death unloads; it can create more wants than it satisfies, for the universe does not have sufficient resources to satisfy all the desires that only one person may possibly have. When one achieves power, there still may be unanswered questions: what is to be done with the power to achieve happiness? To achieve and maintain fame, one may have to conform continuously to a fickle changing opinion of the public. Is this happiness? The satisfaction of sensual pleasure often is followed by extreme melancholy, giving temporary gratification but not necessarily happiness. There are many examples of individuals who have sought and found wealth, power, fame, and sensual pleasure, but who do not appear to have found happiness. Some questions that may be asked about happiness are: is it a necessary reciprocal; that is, does one have to give it to receive it? Do we wish to be happy, or just happier than others? Can happiness be achieved by adjusting to being without it? How do we measure the quality of happiness? These questions, and many more, must be answered before one is prepared to strive for happiness; and these questions cannot be answered by the mere striving. Again, some outside standard and/or means are needed.

Chapter Three

Definitions and Basic Assumptions

An assumption is defined as that which is accepted as true. The foundation of all thinking and communication involves knowledge of what assumptions are being used. The major form of communication is by the use of words, for which we use definitions which are assumptions stating the meaning of the words. The same word may, in ordinary usage, have numerous different and acceptable meanings, depending upon the context in which the word is used. In ethical discourse, it is important to have an accepted integrated set of definitions with each word having a single unambiguous meaning. Also, ordinary dictionaries do not provide definitions that adequately clarify the meanings of very complex concepts such as truth, good, justice, etc., and lengthy supplemental essays are needed for an understanding of the concepts. It is also important in stating definitions to avoid inadequacies such as the following:

Circulatory- using the word (or derivative of or a synonym) being defined in the definition (e.g. "patriotism is a feeling shown by a patriot").

Negativity- defining something as being the negative of something else, which also has not been defined, or stating it is not something (e.g. "an automobile is not a tree") yet leaving a host of possible things which it is.

Obscurity- ambiguous, metaphorical or unintelligible definitions (e.g. "love is a difficult complex maintenance of individual integrity throughout the incalculable process of inter-human polarity").

Incongruity- using definitions which are either too broad or too narrow to distinguish the word being defined (e.g. defining a "pencil" as "a writing instrument" is too broad as the definition also includes pens; defining a "pencil" as "a writing instrument made out of wood and lead" is too narrow as it excludes automatic pencils made out of other materials.

Extraneousness- stating unique complex attributes or properties that do not give the essentials needed for a clear understanding of the word being defined (e.g. "a circle is a figure having an area equal to pi times the square of the radius"). Such a definition is unlikely to aid one in recognizing a circle.

Chapter 6 attempts to provide an integrated set of definitions of words commonly used in ethical discourse, each with a single unambiguous meaning, along with some 50 essays related to words which were deemed to need additional clarification of their meanings, or relevant discourse.

The foundation of ethical discourse in deciding what is right or wrong, is an assumption of the purpose of human existence. That which is ethical or right fulfills the purpose of human existence. If we assume there is no purpose to human existence, than any action is acceptable; there is no right or wrong.

The assumption or determination of the purpose of human existence cannot be determined by scientific experiments, as it is a metaphysical or ontological problem which must be solved by analogical inference and logical argument. Man ascribes purposes to his body parts (e.g. the purpose of the eye is to see; the purpose of the ear is to hear), but generally has difficulty ascribing a purpose for the entire being. Some have proposed the following as man's purpose: the attainment of happiness, the attainment of power, or the preparation for a life hereafter. However, these "beg to question" mere statements do not indicate how one attains happiness, what one would do with power once attained, or how one prepares for the life hereafter.

A means of finding a logical answer to the question is to assume that the "ultimate gift of existence" is available, and then consider what would be desirable ways to occupy time or fulfill the purpose of existence. The "ultimate gift of existence" is defined as having available, just for the asking, any material things in any quantity desired. Thus, there would be no need to work for a living as anything money could buy would be available in unlimited quantities. Part of everyone's time each day would be not need to be occupied by the requirements to maintain the existence of the individual and of the human race, including such activities as eating, sleeping, physical activity, (sports), sex, etc. When desired activities, other than those required to maintain existence, are identified, it is logical to assume that these other activities are the reason for or the purpose of maintaining existence. Such a list of desired activities, beyond those required to maintain existence, may be generated by noting the admired activities of great men and those of individuals fortunate enough to have leisure time. Such a list of desired activities would include such actions as to discover, learn, invent, build, perform, travel, heal, teach, improve, serve, conserve, provide, protect, produce, solve, and create. All of these actions could be placed in the general categories of the *search for and dissemination of truth and helping others*. Voltaire stated this purpose of human existence very succinctly: "To discover what is true and to practice what is good." The proposals that "beg the question" are thus illustrated as those activities that will also provide the means of attaining happiness, reasons for desiring power, and generally, would be considered to be a proper preparation for the life hereafter.

Agreement on the purpose of human existence is a necessary basic assumption, for a course of action that is "right" must be consistent with this basic assumption and fulfills the purpose of human existence. The writer, working together with others, has found the following additional basic assumptions to be reasonably acceptable and to serve rather effectively as the foundation for discourse and problem solving in the area of ethics; (these are based upon society as it ought to be, not is).

1. *Man and the universe exist and will continue to exist*. This assumes that there is a reality, and all is not, for example, a figment of man's imagination. Also, this statement assumes that this reality will continue to exist for the foreseeable future, although there may be evolutionary changes occurring.
2. *Each man should expect to live for the average statistical life-span, and each period of this anticipated life has equal value*. This assumes that the future, although indefinite and uncertain, should not be sacrificed for the present which is only one moment in the total span.
3. *Every man has a purpose (beyond mere existence), and every man must be given equal opportunity to fulfill this purpose*. A corollary of the latter part of the above assumption is that every man has some worth alive; no life is to be intentionally destroyed. One often hears arguments that we should encourage evolutionary preservation of the strong and destruction of the weak. "Why not kill off (or use medical experimentation) the incurably ill, the feeble, the insane, the immoral and use the natural resources thereby saved to aid others?" If such ideas were carried to their extremes and society did not protect the weak and feeble, the human race would be destroyed, for who are the weakest and most feeble but the babies? Who would decide who was to be destroyed? Private revenge and crime could creep into the decision making. Cures for the "incurable" may be brought forth any day. If the purpose of the eye is to see, we do not expect any one eye to see everything there is to see or all eyes to see equally well; nor should we condemn any man for similar failings. The man with one arm may teach us all how to make more effective use of each of the arms we have. It should be our obligation to encourage and protect the individuality of each man in his attempt to fulfill his purpose.
4. *No man, nor the human race, can know all of reality (all truths, and therefore, should be most concerned with those truths which have the*

greatest generality, particularly those involving the individual and social existence of man. This assumption indicates that if we wish to seek, to correlate, and to disseminate truths and recognize that there is not enough time in a lifetime to seek all truths, we ought first to attempt to decide (assume) whether or not all truths have equal value, and if not, determine a means of discrimination. Ordinarily, we would be less concerned with determining random, uncorrelated truths, such as counting the number of blades of grass in a specific square foot of the front lawn or counting the number of grains of sand in a cubic foot of earth underneath the grass, then we would be in determining the general characteristics of all blades of grass or all grains of sand. The correlation between several truths is also more important than the finding of an isolated truth.

5. *Life, property, and freedom are inalienable rights of every man.* This assumption indicated that the ideal state shall not have the right to take a man's life under any circumstances, take property without due compensation, or prevent his action when it is demonstrated that he acts with reason. To do otherwise is to invite the totalitarian state where no one can be sure that he is not expendable for the "good of the state." A corollary of this assumption is that the state exists for the benefit of man, not man for the benefit of the state.

6. *We should seek to use the least amount of material, energy, and time to fulfill a purpose.* This conforms to natural "laws of conservation of energy."

7. *When a problem does not involve appraisal of major or radical changes in the existing social order, it shall be assumed that the existing social order is to be maintained, with allowances for gradual evolutionary changes.* Most ethical problems must be solved within the framework of an existing social order, and these problems are not likely to have any major immediate effect on the social order.

Chapter Four

Principles and Rules

Principles such as Kant's Categorical Imperative should be followed or applied to all actions, if an individual wishes to be consistently ethical. However, ethical rules only need to be generally followed, with exceptions to be made when adequately justified. Ethical rules can give us ready, tried precepts of reason which may be memorized or quickly looked up to help insure the correct action. Ethical rules may be placed in three classifications:

1. Fundamental rules-rules that apply to all people (e.g. "do not break a promise");
2. Local rules-rules which apply only to certain groups (e.g. codes of ethics applying to the practice of engineering, medicine, or law);
3. Neutral rules-rules which could apply equally well if the opposite was chosen (e.g. "drive on the right side of the road"), but some choice must be made so that people may expect and rely on conformity.

Ethical rules are established, justified, modified (and occasionally may be broken) by application of ethical principles. One should know the intent or purpose behind a rule and how it fits into a system of rules, for proper application. The complicated nature of human affairs prevents ethical rules from being framed without any exceptions. Certainly a promise to take a child to the circus should be broken if the child develops a 105° temperature even if the child still desires to go to the circus. Ethical rules can differ, even be opposite, in different geographical or social conditions, yet both may be justified by the same principle. Ethical rules intended for ordinary men should not be too far beyond the capacities of ordinary men in ordinary occasions or there may be a general breakdown in compliance (e.g., prohibition), and thus adversely affecting compliance with other rules. On the other hand, rules which will generally receive compliance only from saints or heroes (e.g., "turn the other cheek") can set an example or goal for ordinary men, and other rules may be changed in this direction as the level of ethics of the ordinary man rises. This writer believes that the ethical principle Kant's Categorical Imperative (the Universal Law) is by far the best available tool for teaching and solving ethical problems; and it is the only principle used in the presentation of the *Problem Solving Procedure*. Kant's Fundamental Principles of the Metaphysics of Morals is very ponderous and difficult to understand. His statement of the Categorical Imperative "Act as if the maxim of thy action were to become by thy will a universal law of nature" is also difficult to understand, and undoubtedly a major reason it is essentially unknown to the general public. However, when the Categorical Imperative is fully understood and utilized, it becomes evident that it is one of the great thoughts of all time.

The Universal Law involves a consideration of what would happen if everyone in the universe were to do as you propose to do. Right and wrong, if they are to have any meaning, must have the same meaning for everyone. It is absurd to say that what is right for one person would under the same conditions be wrong for another, as it is to expect the laws of gravity to apply to some but not to others. Wrongdoing is making an exception for oneself. Each person should obey the same rules he wants others to obey. The person who commits a wrong act adopts one course of action for himself, but he wants others to follow a different one. Thus, if all people were thieves, there would be no private property available to meet one's needs. The thief wants special privileges in which he is the only one that can steal. Similarly, in the case of the liar, if all men told lies, there could be no communication or trust of any man, thus leading to a break down of society. The Categorical Imperative indicates that it is one's duty to follow the course of action made evident when universalizing of the action results in a social condition which is consistent and rational.

Chapter Five

Problem Solving Procedure

After one has used this procedure a number of times it should be possible, for many situations, to determine right or wrong or what ought to be done by going quickly through the procedure mentally. However, when first using the procedure and for any complex situation, it is best to go through the three steps in writing as shown in the following example solutions. In very complex situations, it may be desirable to take considerable time (to sleep on it) and to request help in making "predictions" from others willing to help, before completing the "analysis." The three step methodology is outlined as follows:

1. State clearly the existing situation and proposed course of action.
2. Magnify the situation. Predict the resultant situation or condition or the type of society that would exist if everyone in the universe, in the same original situation, were to follow or use the same proposed course of action.
3. Analyze the predictions to determine whether or not the resultant situation or condition or type of society would be desirable or beneficial, would be a society that could function effectively, and whether or not it is consistent with the basic assumptions in Chapter 3.

EXAMPLE SOLUTIONS

The first example solution is for a situation where breaking the law is justified. The second and third examples include situations which appear similar, but one is ethical (right) and the other is not. Additional example solutions follow for a diverse set of situations.

Example 1

Situation and proposed course of action

An individual in urgent need of medical attention at a hospital is being driven in an automobile which comes to an intersection just after a green traffic light turns red. The proposed course of action is to violate the law and immediately go through the red light and cautiously cross the intersection.

Prediction of resultant situation if everyone in the universe, in the same situation, were to follow the proposed course of action

Many lives would be saved by the decreased time to reach the hospital. No one would be harmed by the law being broken.

Analysis

The resultant predicted situation is desirable and beneficial and consistent with the basic assumptions. The proposed course of action is ethical (right).

Example 2

Situation and proposed course of action

An engineer is employed and adequately compensated to design a building. A cement manufacturing company offers the engineer a 10% commission on the cost of the cement going into the building if the engineer specifies (requires) that only their brand of cement can be used for the building. The proposed course of action is to accept the 10% commission and specify their brand of cement.

Prediction of resultant situation if everyone in the universe, in the same original situation, were to follow the proposed course of action

A monopoly would be created and the cement company could charge whatever price it wished, thus reducing the ability of everyone to build. A society is sanctioned (approved) where all businesses would seek to please only those with influence and not the ultimate consumer.

Analysis

The resultant situation and type of society are not desirable. The resultant society could not function effectively and the resultant situation is not consistent with the basic assumptions. The proposed course of action is not ethical (wrong). Note: Sometimes situations are distorted by the use of words describing the situation with meanings that are not applicable. In this instance, the offer of 10% is not a "commission" (defined as money received for selling a product or service) but is a "bribe" (defined as money received for the use of undue influence).

Example 3

Situation and proposed course of action

An engineer owner of a contracting firm is planning to submit a bid to obtain a contract to construct a building. He is hoping to be the low bidder who would obtain the contract. A cement manufacturing company offers the engineer a 10% commission on the cost of the cement going into the building. If the engineer would specify (require) the use of their brand of cement in his bid. The proposed course of action of the engineer is to accept the 10% commission and to lower his bid by the savings in the cost of the cement, to increase the probability of being the low bidder.

Prediction of resultant situation if everyone in the universe, in the same original situation, were to follow the proposed course of action

If all manufacturers gave the maximum possible commissions (discounts which are consistent with efficient operations and a reasonable profit) and all contractors submitted the lowest possible bids (consistent with their actual costs plus a fair profit), the maximum amount of goods and services would become available to society.

Analysis

The resultant situation and type of society are desirable. The resultant society can function effectively and the resultant situation is consistent with the basic assumptions. The proposed course of action is ethical (right). Note: Here again is an original situation which is distorted by the use of words with meanings that are not applicable. In this instance, the offer of 10% is not a "commission" (defined as money received for selling a product or service), but is a "discount" (defined as a reduction in price given as an inducement to purchase).

Example 4

Situation and proposed course of action

A young student observes a good friend vandalizing their school building. The student is torn between the obligations to the school and to friendship, but finally decides not to say or do anything that might get the friend in trouble.

Prediction of the resultant situation if everyone in the universe, in the same original situation, were to follow the proposed courses of action

No school could function effectively in vandalized buildings. Vandals not exposed would continue to vandalize, and needed rehabilitation that would make the vandal a better citizen would not take place.

Analysis

The resultant situation and type of society are not desirable. The resultant society could not function effectively and the resultant situation is not consistent with basic assumptions. The proposed course of action is not ethical (wrong). Relations with the friend could be eased by an anonymous report of the vandalism to the authorities.

Example 5

Situation and proposed course of action

A young man accepts a position with an employer whom he does not know very well. After a short time, he discovers that his employer is dishonest, although he has never asked the young man to engage in any crooked action himself. The young man decides to resign and seek another position, even though jobs are scarce at this time.

Prediction of the resultant situation if everyone in the universe, in the same original situation, were to follow the proposed course of action

All dishonest employers would be unable to retain employees. Employees would avoid having their reputations affected by long term association with dishonest employers.

Analysis

The resultant situation is desirable and consistent with the basic assumptions. The proposed course of action is ethical (right).

Example 6

Situation and proposed course of action

A young man is given an assignment by his supervisor to collect some factual data in another city. Upon review of the young man's report, the supervisor, who has many more years of experience, asks the young man to change the report so that it no longer reflects the conditions observed by the young man. The young man decides to make the changes requested by his supervisor.

Prediction of the resultant situation of everyone in the universe, in the same original situation, was to follow the proposed course of action

A society is sanctioned in which all decisions are based upon opinions instead of verifiable facts. A society is sanctioned where all supervisors overrule their subordinates without having verifiable facts. A society is sanctioned where people in power can change data for self-serving purposes.

Analysis

The resultant situation and types of societies are not desirable. The resultant societies could not function effectively and are not consistent with the basic assumptions. The proposed course of action is not ethical (wrong). Note: A proper course of action would be to revisit the site and have a witness at the site confirm the date.

Example 7

Situation and proposed course of action

A senior college student receives invitations to visit two different companies for job interviews on successive days, both companies being located in the same distant city. Both companies send checks to cover all expenses, including round-trip plane fare. The student decides to notify both companies of the situation and return one-half of each check to the companies.

Production of the resultant situation if everyone in the universe, in the same original situation, were to follow the same proposed course of action

A society is sanctioned where all recruiting costs are reduced. A society is sanctioned where all prospective employees consider the welfare of their prospective employers, prior to employment.

Analysis

The resultant types of societies are desirable and could function effectively and consistently with the assumptions. The proposed course of action is ethical (right).

Chapter Six

Definitions and Essays

This chapter includes an integrated set of words, and their definitions or statements of meaning, which are commonly used in ethical discourse. A single unambiguous meaning is given for each word. The definitions are stipulative in that often the meanings are not those of ordinary usage, but are given a meaning which appears best for application to ethical discourse. Most of the words can be adequately defined with a single phrase or sentence. However, many complex words require supplemental essays to clearly understand the meaning of the word, so that it may be used effectively in ethical discourse. The chapter also includes some 50 essays related to specific definitions. The definitions that have related essays are marked with an asterisk (*). The essays alone will provide much food for thought and discussion along a wide range of subject matter.

*ADDICTION–Habitual inclination
ANGER – the desire whereby, through hatred, we are induced to injure someone or something
APPETITE – an impulse or endeavor to modify the body and/or mind
APPROVAL – love towards one who has done good to another or towards something considered good
ASSUMPTIONS – that which is accepted as true
AVARICE – the excessive desire and love of riches
BEAUTY – a measure of the capacity to give pleasure
BELIEF – an individual or minority group's approximation or interpretation of a specific reality
BENEVOLENCE – the desire to do good for others
BLACKMAIL – to force by threats
BRIBE – money received for the use of undue influence
*CAPITAL PUNISHMENT – the death penalty for a crime

*CAUSE – the agent or force producing an effect
*CHARITY – that which is given to help the needy
COMMISSION – money received for selling a product or service
CONCEIT – the attributing to oneself of a perfection which is not there
CONFIDENCE – pleasure arising from an idea where cause of doubt as to the issue has been removed
CONSCIENCE - acquired knowledge that certain acts are approved and rewarded, while other acts are disapproved and punished
CONSEQUENCE – the effects of a specific course of action which can be appraised and evaluated by contemporary reasoning
*COURAGE – the desire to do something good, which others who are equal, fear to attempt
COURTESY – the desire to act in a way which should please others, and refrain from that which should displease them
COWARDICE – the checking of desire by the fear of some danger which others, who are equal, dare to encounter
CRUELTY – the desire whereby a man is impelled indifferently to injure other beings
*DEMOCRACY – rule of the people or possession of the supreme power by the body of the people
DESIRE – a conscious impulse or endeavor to modify the body and/or mind
DESPAIR – a pain arising from an idea where cause of doubt as to the issue has been removed
DEVOTION – love toward something which we admire or respect
DISAPPOINTMENT – pain accompanied by the idea of something past, which has had an issue contrary to our hope
DISCOUNT – a reduction in price given as an inducement to purchase
*DISCRETION – exercising caution and sound judgment
DISPARAGEMENT – hatred in so far as it induces a man to injure by unfavorable comparison
DUTY – the conduct or action required of a person by ethical considerations
*EDUCATION – a process of developing the rational (reason) and creative faculties
EMOTION – the modifications of the body whereby the active power of the body, and the ideas of such modifications, are increased or diminished
EMULATION – the desire to equal or surpass another
*ENDS – the purpose of an action
ENVY – hatred, in so far as it induces a man to be distressed by another's good fortune, and to rejoice in another's bad fortune
*EQUALITY – the same or identical

ESCAPE – gratification or pleasure obtained by temporary avoidance or ignoring of the proximate cause of suffering or pain
ETHICS – the science of determining values in human conduct (what ought to be done)
*EVIL – that which, in accordance with reason, is a hindrance to us in the attainment of any good
*EXPERT – one who has special skill or knowledge
*FASHION – the mode of dress or manners prevailing in society
*FATALISM – the doctrine that all events are irrevocably predetermined so that human efforts cannot alter them
FEAR – an inconstant pain arising from the idea of something past or future, where to a certain extent, we doubt the issue
FREEDOM - a state in which all endeavors are led by reason
FREE-WILL – the doctrine that man has the power to choose between alternatives without necessary compulsion of circumstances or motive
*GAMBLING – taking a risk to obtain a result
*GOOD – that which, in accordance with reason, contributes to existence and/or aids in the accomplishment of man's purpose
GOVERNMENT – the authoritative administration of the affairs of a nation, state, city, etc.
GRATIFICATION – an interpretation of the attainment of (immediate) pleasure, determined solely by application of the physical senses
GRATITUDE – the desire whereby we endeavor to benefit others who, with similar feelings of love, have conferred a benefit on us
GRIEF – pain arising from contemplation of some good we have lost with no hope for recovering it
*HABIT – a relatively fixed mode of activity developed by repetition
*HAPPINESS - a state in which good is being accomplished
HATRED – pain, accompanied by the idea of an external cause
*HISTORY – the branch of knowledge concerned with past events
*HONESTY – the intent to act in accordance with truth and justice
HONOR – pleasure accompanied by the idea of some action of our own, which we believe to be approved by others
*HOPE – an inconstant pleasure, arising from the idea of something past or future, where we do not yet know the issue
IDEA – a mental conception
IDEAL – a concept of an ultimate good, as developed by reason
IMAGINATION – an idea of things not currently present to the physical senses
INDIGNATION – hatred towards one who has done injury to another or towards something considered evil
*INDIVIDUALISM - personal independence in action and thought

INTELLECTUALISM – the endeavor to achieve good beyond that of satisfying self-interest
INTENT – the purpose of an endeavor
JOY – pleasure accompanied by the idea of something past, which has had an issue beyond our hope
JUDGMENT – an endeavor to determine the extent of good or truth in a specific set of circumstances
*JUSTICE- an endeavor in the direction of the greatest good
*KNOWLEDGE – the summation of acquired correlated truths
*LIBERTY – a state in which all endeavors are led by reason
*LOVE – pleasure accompanied by the idea of an external cause (a decision)
LUXURY – excessive desire of possessions
*MATURITY – a relative measurement of adjustment to one's environment
*MEDITATION – to continuously consider thoughtfully
* METAPHYSICS – the systematic study of the fundamentals relating to the ultimate nature of reality and of human knowledge
*MISTAKE – a fault in action or an unacceptable amount of error
MONOPOLY – the exclusive control of a commodity, service or means of production in a particular market
MOTIVE – that which prompts an endeavor
*NEEDS – the necessities of life
*NON-LETHAL WEAPONS – weapons that temporarily incapacitate
*NON- SECTARIANISM – not restricted to or associated with any one religion or sect
*NON–VIOLENT – to eliminate the use of abusive force
ONTOLOGY – the systematic study of the ultimate problems of the reality or being
PAIN – a decrease, as evaluated by reason, in the power to act towards good
PANTHEISM – the doctrine that the entire universe is God
*PATRIOTISM – devotion to principle
PLEASURE – an increase, as evaluated by reason, in the power to act towards good
*POLITICS – an endeavor to build a social structure in which there will be the greatest harmony between men, applications of justice, and commanding positions occupied by the intellectually and morally elite
*POWER – the ability to act
REALITY – that which is, was, or will be
REASON – a process of evaluation using orderly, systematic thinking, aided by the best available instruments for physical measurements, computing devices, and the best judgments of others

REPENTANCE – pain accompanied by the idea of one's self as cause
REVENGE – the desire whereby we are induced to injure one who has injured us
RIGHT – ethical
SANCTION – approve
SHAME- pain accompanied by the idea of some action of our own which we believe to be disapproved by others
*SUCCESS-achievement of progressive good
SUFFERING- an interpretation of the recipient of pain, determined solely by application of the senses
SYMPATHY- love, in so far as it induces a man to feel pleasure at another's good fortune and pain at another's bad fortune
TEMPERANCE- the total abstinence from actions or products which may be injurious to oneself or others
*TIME- the duration measure for everything, with a beginning and an end between a past and future which reaches into the realms of infinity
TIMIDITY- the fear whereby one is induced to avoid an evil by encountering a lesser evil
*TOLERANCE- allowing without active opposition
*TRUTH- a statement, proposition, or belief having the best (in accordance with contemporary reason) correspondence with a specific reality
*TYRANNY- cruel and unjust use of power
*UNCERTAINTY- a doubtful matter
UNDUE- not justified
*UTOPIA- a society which has ideal practical goals toward which it is continually and effectively striving
VIRTUE- any admirable quality or trait
*VOLUNTEERISM- offering to help without being paid
WILL- a conscious endeavor to modify the mind
WONDER- the conception of anything, where the mind comes to a standstill, because the particular concept has no connection with other concepts
*WORLD GOVERNMENT- a single government (one nation) for the entire world
WRONG- not ethical

ADDICTION

By far the best record of success in "curing" addictions has been achieved by the various 12 step programs such as Alcoholic's Anonymous and Narcotics Anonymous. These programs indicate that the first step to a cure is the recognition by the individual that he does have an addiction, be it alcohol, drugs, obesity, gambling, etc., and that the addiction is making life unmanageable. It is difficult to understand the 12 steps by a mere reading, and attendance at meetings is usually necessary in order to understand the rationale behind the 12 steps.

The fundamental premise is that only the addicts themselves can "cure" the addiction. Criticism and threats of punishment by others are generally to no avail and may only aggravate the problem. In order to affect a "cure," the addicts must change their overall way of life to one that is more rational, and recognize that addiction is generally a futile attempt to anesthetize or avoid painful emotions such as fear, anger, loneliness and shame.

It is too imposing a task to think in terms of changes affecting the rest of one's life. The programs suggest "taking one day at a time." To avoid the addiction for the rest of one's life is imposing; but to avoid the addiction just for today is a readily achievable goal. As a way of life one should consider only the problems that can be solved in one day (today), not all the problems of a lifetime each day.

The number of problems to be solved each day should be reduced to a reasonable amount - many of the problems can be postponed; and many will disappear, if postponed. This very significant means of reducing stress provides a major means of resisting the call of the addiction.

The 12 steps frequently suggest leaving matters to a "higher power." It is left to the individual to decide what they wish to consider as their "higher power" - it may be God, nature, or even the group meeting. As a way of life, one must try to stop worrying about all the tragedies that might happen and are beyond our control - leave these matters to the "higher power" to achieve inner peace; and relieve stress by being prepared to accept that which cannot be changed. Control of anger and hate, and the substitution of love is a more likely means of solving one's problems in a positive manner. When stress is reduced and problems are solved in a positive manner, there is less need and desire for that which causes the addiction.

The group meetings provide continuous support for coping with the addiction. "Sharing" at the meetings of experiences of others provide graphic illustrations of "do's and "don'ts" learned the hard way. "Sharing" of one's own experiences and concerns provide a catharsis and sometimes invaluable suggestions from the members of the group. Members of the group who have been "clean" for a significant period volunteer to serve as a sponsor for newcomers to the group, and serve by providing advice (when asked) and instruction about the programs, on a personal basis, outside of the meetings. Traditions of the group include: the leaders being trusted servants who do not govern and are non-professional; each group is autonomous and fully self-supporting by modest donations; no opinions are to be expressed by the group on issues outside the area of addiction; and anonymity and confidentiality are carefully preserved.

The 12 step programs have also recognized the importance of having relatives and friends of the addict understand the nature of the problem, and they have established separate group meetings such as Al-Anon and Nar-Anon for concerned and affected relatives and friends. One of the primary messages given by these groups to the relatives and friends, or co-dependents, is the three C's: you didn't CAUSE the addiction; you can't CURE it; and you can't CONTROL it. It typically takes quite a few meetings to understand the concept of co-dependent's "enabling" the addict's continuation of the addiction. "Enabling" involves helping the addict get out of the messes he created, or any help which eliminates the negative consequences normally brought on by continuing the addiction. The addict generally has to "touch the stove" to learn that it is hot; and "help" which prevents being 'burned" is enabling continuance of the addiction. Help or support by relatives and friends which contribute to a "cure" are a positive attitude, acceptance, and "tough-love" - hate their vices, but not the addicts. These groups also concentrate on recovery of the co-dependents to give them peace of mind and to learn how to relate to the addict - to love and let be. When the codependents stop trying to dictate the life of the addict and, thereby, making a major change in the addict's environment, there very often is a miraculous change in the addict.

CAPITAL PUNISHMENT

The Declaration of Independence includes one of the greatest concepts developed by civilization: "We hold these truths to be self-evident, that all men are created equal; that they are endowed by their Creator with certain inalienable rights; that among these are life, liberty, and the pursuit of happiness." As used in the Declaration the term inalienable means that which cannot be taken away, either by man or government. The Declaration therefore establishes an ideal to be sought in which no man or government can take away an individual's life, liberty, or pursuit of happiness (without qualification or under any possible circumstances), for these are rights given by the Creator. Unfortunately few, either at the time of the Declaration or today seem to understand the meaning of inalienable, as we may judge from the continued use of capital punishment and of war as a means of resolving disputes. The Declaration of Independence is not part of the U.S. Constitution; and this vital ideal should be made the law of the land by a constitutional amendment adding the statement on inalienable rights to the Bill of Rights.

There are logical arguments which can demonstrate that a well functioning government can meet the ideal of granting these inalienable rights, in all conceivable circumstances without any qualifications. This can easiest be demonstrated in a discussion of capital punishment. For example, the incorrigible criminal might be used as a human guinea pig for medical experimentation. The intent of the experimentation would not be to kill, but if the criminal died, it would be a positive "eye for an eye" with the potential of "replacing" many lives. Is not this alternative better than the mere destruction of a life as demanded by capital punishment? Would this not leave life as an inalienable right, for there is no intention of taking a life under any circumstances? Similarly, intent to kill in self defense is not justifiable; as the intent of self defense should be to prevent injury to oneself. The intent should be to use the least force necessary for defense -- killing of the criminal might happen in self defense, but the intent should be incapacitate not to kill (see also NON-LETHAL WEAPONS). There is always a better more positive alternative than killing (some might justify killing in war; but war itself is never rational or justifiable where tyrants rule; it is rational to incapacitate the tyrant, not to kill through war the subjects under the tyrants rule).

CAUSE

Many claim that every event has a cause, and that the cause of an event is a previous event. Others claim that nothing has a cause; still others claim that some events have causes and others have no causes. When we seek to find the cause of any event we will see that the search ultimately leads to the "absolute" cause of the universe. For example, in seeking the cause of a short-circuit we might find frayed insulation; but then we must seek the cause of the frayed insulation which might be swaying of the wire caused by the wind. Then we must seek the cause of the wind, which ad infinitum will lead to the "absolute" cause of the universe.

It is doubtful if we can ever find the absolute cause of the universe, or the absolute cause of any event, even if they do exist; nor need these absolute causes be of particular concern to the individual. For example, if a scientist or engineer were to come forth and declare in great triumph:

"I have discovered the cause of gravity," the world would be unlikely to pay near as much attention as to a proclamation: "I am able to both produce and prevent gravity." This demonstrates an important principle: we should be interested in causes of an event primarily in the sense that the cause is one of its conditions which we are able to produce or prevent.

The following is an example related to the above principle: A car skids and overturns while going around a curve. From the driver's point of view, and ability to prevent future accidents, the cause was excessive speed and the remedy is more careful driving. From a highway engineer's point of view, and ability to prevent, the cause (or condition) might be the improper design of the curve in the road. From the auto manufacturer's point of view, and ability to prevent, the cause (condition) might have been a center of gravity that is too high. If all involved make the contribution that they are able, considerable progress will be made toward preventing future accidents. Conversely, if each felt that the cause or condition was one that only someone else could prevent, the result would be that nothing would be done.

One of the great problems of our society is that too many are always asking: "Why don't they do something about it," instead of seeking the causes or conditions which they themselves can make contributions toward preventing or producing. We are all capable, at least in some small way, of treating the causes of most events for which we have a concern; and this is our obligation -- not someone else's.

CHARITY

Every good act may be considered to be charity. Even if we have no bounty to share we can give wise counsel, enliven with our presence, give deference to parents, set an example for a child, remove a stone from the road or smile to a stranger.

If we are fortunate to have personal wealth, there is often a quandary to determine how much may be shared and how much should be set aside so that an emergency does not leave oneself in need of charity. Undoubtedly, this quandary is the reason that so much charity is posthumous; thus solving the problem, by insuring there will be no lifetime period when wealth is not at hand. The negative side of large posthumous charities is the loss of seeing gifts enjoyed, and large sums given at once often ruins heirs who have no experience or appreciation of the obligations of wealth. Among the obligations of wealth, when there are so many in need of mere survival, should be to avoid "high" living and to husband and use the wealth wisely.

Charity, whenever feasible, should be given directly; and one should not pay to have the charity distributed by others, who often see themselves as the primary needed beneficiary. A major additional charitable endeavor could come from elimination of wasted crop surpluses and second quality crops, which could be provided to the needy if there were assurances that these crops would not be diverted to the marketplace and volunteers were organized to pick up and distribute the crops. Millions upon millions of needed charitable deeds could come from organized volunteerism (see VOLUNTEERISM).

Tax generated funds should not be utilized to support non-profit organizations, except in emergencies. Non-profit organizations are often a device to gain power and high salaries in a relatively unregulated situation. Tax generated funds given to a non-profit organization forces the public to support charities favored by politicians, who are pressured by paid lobbyists to establish ever higher and higher taxes for this support. Although the titles of the non-profit organizations receiving tax support may reflect worthy services, the taxes utilized leave less funds available for charities which may be much more deserving. If the services performed are vital, then the government should perform it directly and not pay relatively unregulated organizations to perform the services.

Foreign aid, as another category of charity, should be based upon the parable of the fish: "Give a person a fish today, and he will be hungry tomorrow. Teach him how to fish and he will never be hungry." Foreign aid, other than for immediate disasters, should be only for technical assistance or loans backed by collateral. Foreign aid (particularly the World Bank) and favorable trade reciprocity should be related to efforts toward population control, as we are in imminent danger of reaching the effective capacity of the planet. No foreign aid should be given to countries with armies, and no evidence of danger of invasion (police forces should be reasonably proportional to the population, and locally controlled).

COURAGE

Courage may be defined as the desire to do something good which others, who are equal, fear to attempt. Courage does not involve merely the taking of risks; but also the ability to discriminate between what should be undertaken in spite of peril or pain. A man, who drinks polluted water, without knowing it, is taking a risk; but he is not performing what we would call a courageous act. Animals which have no fear of dangers, because they are ignorant of them, are not courageous; they are only fearless and senseless. Courage involves knowledge of the risk not hidden by ignorance or emotional excitement, and a calm appraisal that the worthiness of the cause justifies the risk. It is necessary to know what things should be feared, when they should be feared, and how much. Courage is a golden mean between overconfidence and excess caution. In order to act habitually in a courageous manner each action should be both wise and with a noble goal.

DEMOCRACY

In one of its meanings, democracy flourished in the Greek City-states as early as the fifth century B.C.; while in another, democracy only began to exist in recent times or perhaps does not yet exist anywhere in the world. To decide which of the above is true, it is necessary to understand the ideals of democracy; and comparisons with alternative forms of government are essential: monarchy (decisions by an individual receiving power by inheritance), dictatorship (decisions by an individual receiving power by military force or election under assumed crisis conditions), oligarchy-aristocracy (decisions by a group receiving power based upon status resulting from birth, wealth, or assumed abilities).

There are two forms of democratic government: direct, and representative or republican democracy. Direct democracy is only feasible for small constituencies such as local government town-meetings. For the larger constituencies, practicality requires the delegation of authority to elected representatives. Democracy, when compared to the alternative forms of government, is the form most likely to function to serve and benefit all the people, not merely for one or several groups of them. The definition of democracy infers the above: "rule of the people or possession of the supreme power by the body of the people.'

In our complex urbanized society most democratic government is in the representative form, with relatively little direct democracy. Representative democracy can become dangerously paternalistic if too much emphasis is placed upon the decisions related to which leaders are to be selected, and other major decisions are left primarily in the hands of the elected leaders. The danger of paternalism lies in conceiving benevolence in terms of the will of the benefactor rather than the will of the beneficiary. The intent of democracy is to give the people what they want instead of what the government wants for them. It does not follow that placing power in the hands of a wise and virtuous leader would always ensure a good performance of the duties of government. This would only be possible if the leader was all-seeing, always informed correctly, and was able to discern and always choose honest and competent men to assist in management of the affairs of government. A democracy must depend primarily upon the reasoning of its individuals for its authority and not become overly dependent upon its leaders. Only the individual directly concerned can adequately fit the conclusion to the evidence within the context of his own experience and thought. Only the individual can establish an order of preference and determine which of a range of alternatives can serve him best. Often the leaders themselves not facing the ordinary people's daily struggles for existence, particularly after a long period in office, lose perspective and need the people to reestablish their priorities.

Elected representatives face the difficult task of balancing their function as a messenger for their constituents and the need for independent judgment to decide what is to be done for the common good. It is not always easy to interpret the message of the majority of the constituency and distinguish it from the strident voices of minority special interests. Conversely, sometimes it may be necessary to screen out the superior force of an overbearing majority to support a more worthy minority position. Democratic leaders should be primarily concerned with protecting the rights of individuals and less with protecting the government or state; for institutions are made for man, not man for institutions. A state is just an arbitrary fictitious grouping of real estate, and individuals should not be sacrificed for a fictitious being. Ideally, a democracy should have kind and honest leaders who will respond to 50 or 100 angry people who plead for justice and/or against requests for special privilege.

A well-functioning democracy must provide education for all its citizens which fits them for political freedom, and it must provide for regular, frequent opportunities to participate in government. The citizen's ability to reason must be developed and not be superseded by that of officials acting in the name of the state. Regular, frequent participation in government involves more than voting. In addition to voting, participation may be by involvement in direct democracy (e.g. town meetings), candidacy and encouraging others qualified for candidacy, civic and charitable groups, and volunteerism (see VOLUNTEERISM).

Democracy is in an evolving process with much yet to be done to approach an ideal form of government. The primary problem is that of evolving methods of consistently attracting and electing honest, kind, and competent leaders who communicate with their constituency and are able to develop an efficient and dedicated bureaucracy to assist them (see GOVERNMENT).

DISCRETION

One often sees injustice whose causes lie so deep rooted as to belie any immediate solution. Having seen the madness of the multitude and having also looked into the realms of truth, often there is but one recourse for the individual. It is as though the individual had fallen among wild beasts - he will not join in their viciousness, but neither is he able singly to halt their fierce natures; and reflecting that he would have to throw away his life without doing any good either to himself or others, he holds his peace and goes his own way. He therefore hovers on the outskirts of the pack, seeking the shelter of the surrounding environment. Seeing the rest in their wrong doing, he is content if only he can live his own life honorably and with bright hopes that eventually there may come the support or opportune time to right the situation.

Definitions and Essays

EDUCATION VS. TRAINING

As we give a greater and greater proportion of our population "higher education," there seems to be very little to show for it in vital results such as advances in human interaction and in our relations with our environment. The major fault lies in our being too concerned with the social status accompanying university attendance, while lacking concern about the proper definition or goals of "education."

Education is frequently defined as a process of growth through learning; and the word training is often ascribed to education which prepares one for occupations at the lower levels of social status. This definition of training assumes that the occupations having a lower social status require only a lower level of learning or education. Conversely it thus may be assumed that those wishing to enter endeavors having higher social status will find the necessary "higher education" at the colleges or universities. "Higher Education," under these circumstances, is defined more by its merely being physically located in a university, or by its social status, than by any clear cut difference in the level of learning. "Higher education" or "education" may be distinguished from "training" by the differences in levels of learning, by using the following definitions:

> Education is a process of developing the rational and creative faculties.
> Training is a process of developing the ability to perform a task in a specific manner.

Levels of learning progress from the elementary school where the primary concern is with the mere "memorization" of facts: $2 + 2 = 4$, c-a-t spells cat, etc. As the learning process continues the individual is expected to have committed many facts to memory and also to "understand" how these facts may be applied to situations of varying complexity. "Higher education" should involve primarily the use of reason (rational faculties) to sift the many facts one has "memorized" and/or "understood" to make valid judgments and decisions and to effect vital and creative actions. "Memorization" and "understanding," regardless of the complexity of the concepts, are still essentially elements of "training" in that there is performance in a specifically indicated manner which requires no original or creative reasoning.

Far too many of our university courses require only "memorization," and sometimes "understanding," of names, places, dates, equations, etc. Repetition of subject matter which is ordinarily covered in high school is justified by the use of words with a greater number of syllables or by the introduction of concepts which are more difficult to "understand." The lecture class, in which the only student activity is the absorption and regurgitation of the lecture material on an examination, hardly can be classified as any more than "training." The trend to larger and larger classes must necessarily result in less and less of the individual student participation required for "education." Too many of our universities appear to be satisfied with selling the public "training," with social status.

"Education," as defined herein, requires that the majority of the class activity be undertaken by the student, under the critical supervision of the faculty. Effective reasoning and creativity must be based upon facts which are "understood", and possibly "memorized." "Education" would require that the student obtain experience in isolating the facts needed, from the infinite number of facts available, to carry out a particular reasoning or creative process. "Education" would not have the instructor isolate facts neatly for mere presentation in a lecture, and the good teacher would make himself progressively unnecessary. "Education" requires far more than being well-informed. "Education" would include and evaluate experiences requiring the student to act in accord with order and logic, assent with caution, correct false impressions with readiness, meditate with pleasure, suspend judgment with patience, be free of delusion, speak with modification, and to foresee and to avoid catastrophes.

ENDS AND MEANS

In ordinary usage an end is considered to be something we aim at or choose for its own sake; whereas, means are considered to be methods chosen because of the results yielded. Thus if one walks for health, walking would be considered the means to achieve the end of health.

A commonly heard statement is "The end justifies the means." That is, we can justify any means of accomplishing something, if the end accomplished is considered to be good. Common usage also frequently colors the same means upon the basis of the end achieved, or its justification. Thus when the means are unjustified it is "murder," when the means are justified it becomes "capital punishment," or "military art." The fallacy in "the end justifies the means" should become evident if further analysis is made of these so-called ends and means.

Following a sequence of ends and means, one may attend college as a means of earning a degree as an end. But why does one want a degree? The degree might be considered to be a means of earning a living, as an end. But why does one want to earn a living? Earning a living may be considered a means of continuing to exist, as an end. But why does one want to continue to exist? Other sequences of ends and means could also invariably be led back to this same latter question; that is, it will be found that all of our so-called ends are themselves only means to an ultimate (assumed) end or purpose. We may effectively set for ourselves what may be considered intermediate ends such as earning a degree or acquiring a new home; but it should be recognized that these are only means to achieve an ultimate end or purpose of existence.

In actuality, therefore, means and (intermediate) ends cannot be separated, for the intermediate ends are themselves only means to an ultimate end. In evaluating any action, the total effect of both means and (intermediate) ends must be considered in determining the good; just as we might evaluate the worthwhileness of an intermediate end of spending an afternoon at the beach by considering the total effect, including the means, which may involve a hazardous and wearying drive to and from the beach.

It should therefore be evident that the "end" cannot justify the means, that evil means must never be used under any circumstances. Both the means and intermediate end have an effect upon achieving one's ultimate purpose; and the means can have more effect than the intermediate end. All too often there may be neglect of the effect of the means in weakening the will and character of the individual, or in debasing the social environment - setting up a pattern which later results in attitudes and desires for revenge, cruelty, and ill-will. All is not necessarily well that "ends" well.

EQUALITY

Equality is not a law of nature. It is difficult to find equality in nature - its sovereign law appears to be subordination and dependence. Jefferson proposed an ideal for society to attempt to achieve: "...all men are created equal; that they are endowed by their Creator with inalienable rights; that among these are life, liberty and the pursuit of happiness." Obviously, Jefferson did not propose that all men are created with equal physical, mental and other attributes. However, it is greatly desirable for society to attempt to provide equal rights for all. Unfortunately, little progress has been made in this attempt, for the accidents of birthplace and parentage, the nature of those with power and influence, and the persistence of the individual all affect the ability to obtain these rights. Equality is not a principle to rely upon to attempt to obtain the inalienable rights - we may better rely on the principle of justice to all. Everyone comes closest to equality at his advent upon earth, and when placed beneath it.

We frequently use the terms average, above average and below average; and we place everyone into these categories. Yet there is no feasible means of placing the totality of any individual in these categories for every individual has a multiplicity of attributes including health, wealth, talent, I.Q., character (e.g. honesty, concern for others) and education; and each of these attributes may individually also be placed in the categories of average, above average or below average. Everyone probably has some attributes in each of the three categories; and even the most wise and famous will be found to have some below average attributes, while the most lowly or the handicapped will have certain strengths or above average attributes (e.g. the blind tend to have above average hearing). Let us not seek equality, but let us help each individual seek out and develop his strengths to make the maximum contributions to his own welfare and to our society.

ERROR-MISTAKE

Scientists know that while we strive for perfection, the best we can attain in any measurement is an approximation. They know that it is impossible to do anything or measure anything with zero error or with perfection. Determination of the amount of error depends upon the precision of measurement, and we cannot measure with infinite accuracy. Therefore, we must have tolerance in all things, where tolerance is an acceptable amount of error. When there is too large or an unacceptable amount of error, we call it a mistake. We should be intolerant of mistakes, but we must also recognize that it is not in the power of any individual never to make a mistake. We can only attempt to minimize our mistakes. We can never eliminate all errors and all mistakes, but it is important to realize that while errors cannot be avoided, mistakes can.

We probably gain more wisdom from some mistakes or failures than we do from some successes. We often discover what will do by discovering what will not do. The best way to illustrate a mistake made by others is by example, as in the old saying: "If a crooked stick is before you, you need not explain how crooked it is. Just lay a straight one down by the side of it." A man should never be ashamed to admit that he has been wrong or has made a mistake; it is another way of saying that he is wiser today than he was yesterday.

EVIL

There are physical realities in which no negatives actually exist, such as weight or mass and heat. Thus the concept of "cold does not actually exist; it is merely the absence of a certain amount of the positive element of heat. Similarly, there are advantages in assuming that evil is non-existent, but is only the absence or lack of good. Thus we may consider illness the lack of health, greed the lack of courtesy, hate the lack of love, etc. We can consider the process of civilization as the building of a world of good, starting with nothingness. If we were all blind and deaf and moving about in a confined area, it is to be expected that there would be frequent collisions. Although technological advances have been made, civilization's understanding of man's treatment of man is still in its infancy level of essential blindness. We have barely started on the foundations, as we attempt to build a world of good out of nothingness or ignorance.

The alternate outlook of there being a battle between good and evil or a battle between God or his angels and the Devil promotes negativism and a concept of solving problems by violence. Battles can be lost; but we can never lose if we strive continuously to remove ignorance and build a world of good. Socrates stated: "No man does wrong willingly, but in ignorance of the good."

"We are blind until we see that in the human plan, nothing is worth the making if it does not make the man.

Why build these cities glorious, if man unbuilded goes. In vain we build the world, unless the builder also grows."

EXPERT

To become the world's foremost authority or expert is not necessarily a great accomplishment, as may be seen by the following example. A young recent engineering graduate was given as his first job assignment the task of taking initial measurements of the stream flow in one of the many canals (Canal #523) which crisscross the Everglades. His task was completed at the end of the week and a report filed and accepted. It could therefore be said that this young man, one week after graduation, was the world's foremost authority on the stream flow in Everglades Canal #523. It is quite easy to become the world's foremost authority if one narrows down the area of endeavor sufficiently. Indeed, each and every one of us are already the world's foremost authority in many areas such as in the knowledge of our own personal tastes and amount of personal possessions. It should be evident that the renowned expert in a significant area of endeavor must be rather broadly learned. It is also relatively easy to learn something about many things, but essentially impossible to learn everything about anything.

If one wished to know all there was to know about even a relatively narrow area, it can be demonstrated that one would have to know all there is to know about all matters in the universe. If the young engineer mentioned above wished to know all there was to know about the stream flow in Everglades Canal #523, he would have to know all there was to know about fluid mechanics. Fluid mechanics is involved in many fields of engineering so that it would therefore soon become necessary to know all of engineering and its bases of mathematics and the physical sciences. The stream flow may also be affected by plant, fish and animal life and therefore he should know all there is to know about the biological sciences. The Canal was created by and is used by man so that it becomes necessary to know about man and his social, political, economic, philosophical, legal, medical, psychological and cultural problems. The stream flow is affected by meteorological actions which are in turn affected by the moon and the sun; and, therefore, he must also know all there is to know about these and of all the planets, and galaxies, and ad infinitum.

There is no such being as an all-knowing expert. This probably accounts for the tongue-in-cheek definition of an expert: "an ordinary guy far from home." The expert, who has both an extraordinary depth of knowledge in an area, and also an extraordinary breadth, is rare. Typically, we recognize that the local "expert" does not have this extraordinary combination of depth and breadth; and, not knowing whether or not the "expert" from afar does, we tend to hope so and select the distant "expert." All humans make mistakes, including experts, and any one expert may not come up with the "best" solution to a problem. For these reasons we should not blindly trust any expert. One should utilize his own common sense and experiences to evaluate the expert's recommendations, for one's own breadth of experiences may include relevant ones that the expert lacks.

FASHION AND FAD

Thoreau said: "Every generation laughs at the old fashions, but follows religiously the new." Fashion has been defined as a transitory mode of making or doing things which is usually based upon arbitrary and capricious decisions about matters of trifling import, and it rules most where luxury has made the greatest inroads.

Some individuals attempt to be first in the new fashion to draw attention to themselves. Others feel forced to follow fashions and conform so as not to draw attention to themselves. As soon as a fashion becomes universal, it is out of date; and fashion must be forever new or she becomes bland, dull and commonplace.

Without fashion and vanity, perhaps, people may become slovenly. However, as long as there are cold and nakedness in the land around, excess splendor of dress is unconscionable.

FATE

For those who believe in absolute fatalism or predestination, all events are inevitable as though God wound up a clock or mechanical toy which goes through a predetermined movement until the spring winds down. If one were to question this belief and propose the opposite position of free-will, they would argue that your questioning of the belief in absolute fatalism was also predestined as part of your functioning in the universe. A belief in fatalism can provide a peace of mind and a calmer acceptance of apparent misfortune, with the accompanying belief that everything happens as God willed it, and it will all eventually turn, out to be for the best. On the other hand, a belief in fatalism can result in avoiding responsibility and justifying any and all actions because it is so fated.

Any and all actions can also be justified by a belief in absolute free-will, with the accompanying belief that all events in the universe happen by chance. Very few individuals can find satisfaction in a belief which assumes nothing has a purpose, all events happen by chance or accident, and we are free to act in whatever manner we may choose. Most will find it more satisfying to believe in one of several middle-ground positions between absolute fatalism and absolute free-will, as described below:

One middle-ground position may be illustrated by an analogy related to a chance meeting of old friends at an airport after a separation of many years. This meeting is a chance coincidence of two quite separate and independent lines of action coming from different places, going to the same place under the influence of different predestined causes. Both being at the airport together was entirely chance and unrelated to the causes which determined their independent paths. Thus, a rationale is provided for certain events being fated or predetermined and other events being chance.

Another middle-ground position may be illustrated by an analogy between a corpuscle as a part of a man's body and a man as part of the universe. All of the corpuscles in a man's body have a common function or purpose and their normal actions may be predicted statistically, or considered as predetermined. However, if a local injury occurs to the man's body, the actions of corpuscles in the area of the injury are no longer normal; and the normal (predetermined) life span of the corpuscles may be shortened. Similarly, all of mankind has a common predetermined purpose, and the probability of a common response to certain stimuli can be predicted statistically. However, each individual has the free-well to act differently from the statistically predicted (predetermined) behavior when he deems an alternate action is required to cope with a unique situation, catastrophe, etc.

A broader middle-ground position assumes that the physical world and instincts are predetermined, while man has free-will in the spiritual world, in the use of reason, and in man's creations such as art and the social structure. Whenever bees form a hive, it is formed in the same way by instinct (predetermined). Whereas mankind's creations of buildings, forms of governments and laws etc., are widely diverse because of free-will. Thus it becomes important to recognize where free-will applies, and to recognize that we can control our reactions to things even though we cannot control the things themselves. The Serenity Prayer expresses this position very well: "God grant me the serenity to accept the things I cannot change, the courage to change the things I can, and the wisdom to know the difference."

GAMBLING

Thousands of years ago important decisions often were made by lot, thereby referring the decision to the Gods. Some Italian shops of the 15th Century would have a sack of small presents and invite customers to take a lucky dip. This "lotteria" developed into the present day system of raising money by selling chances on prizes. The "lotteria" system spread over Europe, but it lent itself so readily to fraud that it either became forbidden or was conducted as a state monopoly. Gambling among individuals has tended to be restricted or prohibited as, similarly, fraud by professional gamblers has resulted in individuals losing homes and businesses and even gambling themselves into slavery. Gambling at race tracks and casinos is often justified by their being relatively inaccessible to the poor, and those who come can afford the losses. Some small countries, wishing to control gambling by its citizens, limit admission to casinos to foreign nationals who they feel can afford the losses and where they feel no obligation to affect morals. In recent years, as taxes have reached abusive levels, governments are supplementing taxes by sponsoring lotteries which appeal to both the rich and the poor. These lotteries are often justified by supposed assigning of the lottery income to worthy causes such as education, with the lottery income typically permitting reallocation of the funds previously used for education.

Gambling develops a "something for nothing" attitude and a society which breeds people who sit around hoping they will strike it rich, with little effort on their part. Gamblers rely on rules of thumb that have proved highly successful in other realms of daily life, such as "if at first you don't succeed, try, try, again." Gambling is one realm in which these principles do not work; and this is compounded by the tendency of gamblers to be much better at recalling their wins then their losses. Gambling with other people's money, supposedly held in conservative investments, has recently seen an epidemic of bank and stock brokerage failures. The chronic extreme gambler has an addiction (see ADDICTION) which needs extensive therapy; and a government which sponsors gambling is acting akin to promoting the use of drugs in order to supplement tax income, instead of sponsoring therapy.

It is the utmost hypocrisy for government to generally prohibit individual freedom to gamble, while justifying and encouraging gambling when it is sponsored by the state. Instead of offering the poor the faint hope of striking it rich so that they could leave the misery of the inner city, government should be taking steps to provide the jobs, housing, environmental improvements that would cause the misery to leave. The wealthier gamblers are typically seeking risk and excitement which is missing from their daily routines. Through education, government can point alternate paths to risk and excitement through participation in competitive sports, conservation activities and activities which reduce the frequency of accidents and crime; and for those who need higher levels of risk and excitement, it would be better for the government to encourage sky diving than gambling.

GOOD

If we assume that the universe and man exist and man's purpose for existence is the betterment of the universe, then good may be defined as that which aids in bettering the universe; that is, makes existence possible and fuller for all and aids in the search for and dissemination of truth.

Everyone seeks good in his own interest, but not everyone does so in accordance with sound reason; for most men's ideas of good and desirability are guided by their fleshy instincts and emotions, which involve no thought beyond the present and their immediate object. No man desires anything but what at the time seems good to him; although he may recognize that others, possibly the great majority, consider it evil. No man voluntarily pursues what he considers evil, to prefer evil to good is not human nature; and when there is a choice of several goods, no one will choose the lesser goods if he may have the highest and recognizes which is highest. If a man chooses evil he does so because he is mistaken in his judgment and supposes it to be good. Thus the most vicious assassin may not consider his action a crime, but that he is ridding the world of a tyrant. Similarly the thief may consider that he is taking only that of which he has been deprived by the rich.

If the average four year old child was given the choice of a lollipop now or a $1,000,000 annuity at age 21, it is to be expected that the child would choose the lollipop because he does not have the knowledge or ability to weigh a good 17 years in the future. That which is good must be evaluated in perspective against time - this is where most of us fail in our choice of action. An immediate gain must be weighed against the calculated risk and magnitude of a possible future loss, of all the possible consequences. Acceptance of a bribe or an unfair profit now incurs the risk of future loss or reputation in the community and possible far greater losses in one's lifetime income. Indulging an appetite to excess now has the certain consequence of loss in health in the future. We are quite used to giving up a good now (money) to buy insurance against future possible losses such as that due to fire; giving up an immediate gain may similarly be a most inexpensive insurance against overwhelming losses due to repercussions in the future.

Doing others a good is like putting money in the bank - a long term investment which will pay back greater returns from that moment on or at some future date. Conversely, evil action sets a pattern in one's environment which will eventually cause greater losses to all. It is capable of demonstration that wise men given the some complete set of circumstances would generally choose the same course of action. This, of course, does not imply that all wise men are equal and would themselves be affected the same way by a common stimulus. If one is to achieve the good life, he must first know himself and what kind of events and activities yield experiences that are most valuable. One then learns to predict efficiently the probable total consequences of each act and plan accordingly.

GOVERNMENT

The ideal form of government is a democracy (see DEMOCRACY) where the body of the people possesses the supreme power, where a large percentage of the people are involved in the governmental processes beyond merely voting for their leaders, and where the individuals do not become overly dependent upon their leaders. Good government must be an evolving process working toward realistic ideals. Some of the major goals and needed changes in our current procedures which may lead toward these ideals follow:

1. Seek to provide the best possible educational system (see EDUCATIONAL PRIORITIES); for good government is dependent upon a well-informed citizenry having highly developed abilities to reason, and who are dedicated to truth and justice.
2. Seek to maintain governmental units' at the most efficient population size, and a size which will permit ready contact with and knowledge about the functioning of its leaders. Studies have shown that efficiency of government is a function of size and that the cost of government per capita increases when the size is too small or too large. Participation of the citizenry should be facilitated and encouraged by scheduling public hearings at convenient times such as evenings, weekends, and holidays.

3. Seek to maintain the duties of elected leaders at a level where they can be performed part-time (without personal assistants), and the pay can be small. This is vital if the citizenry is not to become overly dependent upon its leaders; and part-time duties open up candidacy to larger numbers of the citizenry. When political positions become full-time and highly paid, it also becomes very difficult to replace undesirable incumbents who face possible unemployment and a severe loss in income, and who may attempt every possible means of retaining their position.
4. Seek to maintain the smallest possible governmental civil service. This may be done by having government focus primarily on regulation and as little as possible on operations. Very few civil service positions should be full-time, and pay scales should be below that of the private sector so that the individuals attracted will tend to be those who have ideals related to serving the public and who will make financial sacrifices for these ideals and a stable position. The great majority of civil service positions should be filled by unpaid volunteers (see VOLUNTEERISM) and other part-time employees. Although volunteers and part-time employees ordinarily are not as efficient as full-time employees, it is believed efficiency may be compensated by idealism to result in better government than is provided by today's bloated bureaucracy which is reported to be taking about 50% of the earnings of the average individual to support local, state, and federal taxes.
5. Seek to improve the qualifications of candidates for political offices. Current laws regulate and establish minimum standards, before individuals can practice in professions such as law, medicine, and engineering, to protect the public against incompetence and charlatans. Should there not also be equivalent minimum standards to be met in order to hold political office when, in the extreme, individuals can cause economic chaos or bring a nation into war? One practical minimum standard might be a requirement of rising through the ranks (e.g. require prior service as a volunteer or as a member of an appointed board before becoming a candidate for an entry level elected office, require prior service as a mayor before becoming a candidate for governor). Another requirement might limit the term of any one office thus creating an up (to higher responsibility, based upon good performance) or out standard. An ideal to be worked toward is major improvements in the techniques used in character education, and the development of valid and reliable methods of evaluating honesty, emotional stability, etc. of political candidates.
6. Seek to improve election procedures. The following are some changes which appear to be both needed and practical:

a. Reduce the number of voter decisions required on each ballot so that one may be more readily informed (ballots requiring 30 or more decisions are becoming increasingly frequent).
   b. Provide more convenient voting times including more evening hours, weekends, holidays, and by mail.
   c. Reduce the length of time between qualifying and election to keep campaign costs more related to the compensation of the office. The reduced campaign time and financial burdens would also create more competition for the offices.

7. Vary the size of the plurality required for approval of issues, depending upon the importance of the issue and the necessity for speed: the more grave and important the issue, the nearer should the opinion that is to prevail approach unanimity; the more the matter calls for speed, the smaller the prescribed differences in the number of votes may be allowed to become.
8. Ordinarily, issues should not be debated or voted upon on the same day they are introduced. Deferring the question to the next meeting may avoid individuals' defending foolish first-thoughts instead of considering the public good.

HABIT

Every habit or faculty is maintained and increased by the corresponding action: the ability to run is acquired by running. He who has lain in bed for ten days would see how his legs are weakened and the consequences should he afterwards attempt a long run. If then you do not wish to be of an angry temper, do not feed the habit. When you have been angry, this malignity has not only overcome you, but you have increased the habit; you do not reckon only with this single defeat but you have nurtured your incontinence. He who overcomes a habit once, twice, three times weakens it; he who overcomes it many times tends to destroy it.

Generally then if you would make anything a habit, do it; if you would not make it a habit, do not do it, but accustom yourself to do something else in place of it.

HAPPINESS-PLEASURE

It is said that everyone seeks happiness; but what is it that we are seeking? Is it the same for all, or do different people seek different things in the name of happiness? If the pursuit of happiness is not a futile quest, by what means or steps should it be undertaken? The first step needed is to define (definitions are assumptions – see DEFINITIONS) the concepts involved. There are seven different closely interrelated concepts involved, as defined and discussed below:

Definitions

Good- that which, in accordance with reason, contributes to existence and/or aids in the accomplishment of mankind's purpose for existence.
Happiness- a state in which good is being accomplished.
Pleasure- an increase, as evaluated by reason, in the power to act towards good.
Gratification- an interpretation of the attainment of (immediate) pleasure, determined solely by application of the physical senses.
Suffering- an interpretation of the recipient of pain, determined solely by application of the physical senses.
Escape- pleasure of gratification obtained by temporary avoidance or ignoring of the proximate cause of pain or suffering.

Based only upon the use of the physical senses one might receive gratification from food which has in it a tasteless deadly poison; but, in accordance with reason, the sensation must be defined as pain. Conversely, the sensation received while a dentist is drilling a tooth to remove decay may appear to be suffering; but, in accordance with reason, the sensation must be defined as pleasure. A mere statement by an individual that he had pleasure (e.g. "I sure had a good time (pleasure) last night – I was so drunk I don't remember what happened; but I sure had a good time last night") does not necessarily make it so, for the physical senses are most fallible. Our physical senses indicate, for example, that the sun travels around the earth, that the moon changes its shape during each month and that the telephone pole in the distance is much shorter than the pole nearby – these perceptions are corrected by reason.

There are an infinite variety of activities an individual may choose from, each of which may give pleasures of varying quality. Pleasures may be categorized as appetitive, intellectual, or escape. Appetitive pleasure (e.g. eating, sex) have characteristics of being temporary in nature and having diminishing returns (as the amount of activity increases the amount of pleasure received decreases). The intellectual pleasure (e.g. the search for knowledge, friendship) have characteristics of greater permanency and increasing returns (as the amount of activity increases the amount of pleasure increases) Pleasure may be obtained from escape (e.g. a walk in the woods) if one comes back refreshed and inspired with new ability to remove the proximate cause of pain; conversely, escape may bring gratification by dulling the senses to pain by means of drunkenness, but the proximate cause of pain remains.

The greatest happiness comes from choosing the highest quality of pleasures. All three categories of pleasure are needed for a proper balance; but the intellectual pleasures should be dominant, without the usual undue emphasis on pleasures of the appetite and escape.

HISTORY

Most historians of our day have been overly conscientious; in their care not to present a scientific untruth, they have sifted all the evidence until only the dull verifiable facts, (e.g. names, dates, wars) remain. But what these historians forget is that the important historical facts are rarely verifiable for they take place in the mind. The important facts have to do with the passions and motives of men that no one ever sees. The real historical events are decisions, not the consequent motion of arms and legs; but the historian can verify only the leg motion. It is only from a study of these decisions that posterity can learn right and wrong and avoid the errors of the past.

Man has benefited very little from the mistakes of the past because he does not know the reasons. History tells us that Caesar crossed the Rubicon, that was his leg motion, that was verifiable; but why did he cross the river, what were his thoughts, his anxieties, his hopes, his plans? Herein lies the true history. The historian's concern with verifiable precision has too often made history an accurate but lifeless record of secondary data with the omission of whatever made this data vital. We could benefit greatly if there were detailed follow-ups of Pitkin's "Short Introduction to the History of Human Stupidity" to replace much of history's glorification of man's treatment of man.

HONESTY

Honesty is generally characterized as being truthful, law- abiding, fair, and candid. It is doubtful that any individual is absolutely and always honest, and it is not necessarily desirable to be absolutely and always honest. Breaches of honesty are justifiable in certain instances, particularly when there is danger involved and when there is no perceived harm to anyone by the action. Following are some examples in which breaches of honesty may be justifiable:

Breaching of the law requiring stopping at a red light would be justifiable in a life threatening emergency, particularly if care is taken to see that the intersection is free of other traffic.

Stealing the weapons or bombs of a terrorist would be a justifiable breach of honesty.

Helping oneself to minor property from one's workplace (e.g. an envelope, paper clip, rubber band, etc.) may be justified by the convenience provided. The time involved in asking prior permission or arrangements for compensation is not warranted for such minor valued items. Compensation for a significant total over a period of time might be provided by one working overtime, without compensation.

A "white" lie such as Santa Claus bringing the presents, or an enthusiastic assessment of one who has overachieved his normal capacity, is justifiable when the lie does no perceived harm to anyone.

Breaking a promise may be justified in instances such as a life-threatening emergency or where keeping the promise could result in a major economic loss far exceeding any loss incurred by breaking the promise.

A breach of fairness or equity such as the acquisition of an item at a small fraction of its worth may be justified if the seller's acquisition cost was very low and the item has a high value to only a few with special interests (e.g. a special postmark on a common postage stamp, an old fountain pen, a particular beer or cigar label, autographs, etc.). Added to the actual acquisition costs should be the time involved in becoming knowledgeable about the item and time spent in other fruitless searches for similar items.

HOPE

Hope is the universal cure: the captive's freedom, the sick man's health, the lover's victory, and the poor man's wealth. Hope and love are the only goods common to all men. A strong mind always hopes, and always has cause to hope; because it knows the mutability of human affairs, and how slight a circumstance may change the whole course of events. Yet we must recognize that our hopes fulfilled very likely will not be exactly at the time nor in the circumstance we most desire; nor should we magnify the advantages to come.

Of course, we must also recognize that many hopes will be unfulfilled; and to hope for too much is a great obstacle to happiness. When hopes are transformed to worries our burdens are greatly increased. However, it is unlikely that we will sink under the burdens of the day. It is when tomorrow's burdens are added to today's that the weight may be more than can be borne. Taking one day at a time, and sometimes we need to take one hour at a time, is a vital formula for coping. Today is mostly our own, for we can truly see most of what bears upon us; we cannot see what the future may bear.

INDIVIDUALISM

In our striving to achieve an ideal democracy we must singularly tolerate and maintain individualism and guard against regimentation. We must resist the pressure of mere opinion and the fear of being thought to be different. Conformity to customs can preserve the achievements of the past, but we also must be aware that the blind following of customs can result in the continuance of mistakes made by influential leaders. Customs are made by men, and men can change them. It is more important to know how people should act then how they have acted.

The maldistribution of wealth too often binds men to routines of drab simple survival excluding the free play of imagination, thought, and choice which are the most fruitful source of individual differences. A major goal for improved standards of living should be the creation of intervals between one individual and another. Privacy is the greatest of luxuries and a chief condition of individualism. Every large urban area should have nearby stretches of countryside and open spaces largely uninhabited by man. Every family that wants a garden should be able to have one of its own. There should be mandatory buffer requirements (parks, rivers, lakes, etc.) between residential and other land uses.

Individualism infers differences and dictates against comparisons. It is best not to compare oneself with others, because it will only make one vain or bitter. One should consider himself/herself to be a unique individual, beyond any comparison with others.

JUSTICE

Justice may be defined as an endeavor in the direction of the greatest good for a specific set of circumstances. It therefore must be recognized that we all, at times, commit unjust actions through ignorance, neglect, misjudgments, inattention, haste, accident, etc. An ideal system of justice recognizes that no individual is perfect, and it seeks to maximize the number of just actions and minimize the number of unjust actions that take place in a civilized society.

Currently, we attempt to achieve justice by a confused mixture of deterrence, punishment and reform of the criminals. The primary actions are imprisonment and/or capital punishment. Equal justice seems to be based upon the concept of "an eye for an eye, a tooth for a tooth" and the whims of judges and juries in setting punishments. Prescribed punishments then may be modified severely by parole boards and by the lack of sufficient space to house all the criminals. Recently, some concerns have begun to appear related to the rights of victims.

Our penal system is not working if we may judge by the ever increasing crime rate, and very few consider the penal system to be rendering "equal" justice. The current penal system, which is based upon the negative concept of the punishment fitting the crime, should be replaced with a system which is based upon the positive concepts of restitution and reform. The victims would no longer be virtually ignored, but the extent of injury to the victim would be the primary basis of the responsibility for restitution imposed by the judges and juries upon the criminals. Thus the judges and juries would evaluate a dollar equivalent of the injuries to the victim and enforce the compensation of the victim by the criminal. In addition to compensating the victims (whether individual, corporation or government) each criminal would be expected to compensate for his proportionate share of the costs of operating the entire justice system, including police. The first time, non-violent offender might be permitted to carry the responsibilities for compensation without being imprisoned. For those who do not carry out their responsibilities or who are unlikely to carry out their responsibilities for compensation, imprisonment and forced labor would be required; with additional compensation required for the cost of food, shelter, etc. of the prisoner. The prison term would be a function of the earnings of the criminal, and the term could be shortened by the inmate working sixty to eighty hours per week. Instead of capital punishment and the negative concept of taking a life when a life has been taken, the system of justice would require inasmuch as possible the replacement of life (see CAPITAL PUNISHMENT).

Attempts at reform through an educational process must also be an important part of a well-functioning system of justice. Vocational training could both increase the earning capacity of the criminal while in prison and thereby shorten the prison term, and it could increase self- esteem and the ability to function positively in society after completing a prison term. In addition to vocational training, the system of justice should provide what might be called 'character education." Successful examples of this type of education may be found in the educational programs of Alcoholic Anonymous and the ethics education prescribed by many of the professions such as law and medicine. The professions often prescribe additional educational requirements relative to ethics for those members who violate the code of ethics. The educational twelve step program of Alcoholics Anonymous, in addition to assisting in overcoming addiction, recognizes the need to change life styles to cope better with the everyday problems of living.

Alternative methods of dispute resolution such as mediation and arbitration should be encouraged as a substitute for litigation in the courts. These alternative methods provide economy, privacy and speed that are not available through litigation.

KNOWLEDGE

Were it possible to have any one gift that one could think of, as a wish granted by a genie, what would or should that wish be: "All-seeing knowledge."

All-seeing knowledge. Thus we are ignoring a wish or desire for riches, but riches could easily be attained with such intellectuality. Yet the now wise man would not desire riches knowing that whatever he possesses of such a transitory nature will be coveted by others and make for a difficult social existence. By our wish we have ignored our desire for power, but in knowledge we have an irresistible power which carries everything before it. By our wish we have ignored our desire for true friends, but the wise man will have no difficulty in making and keeping friends. By our wish we have ignored our desire for health, but the wise man will be able to do near miracles in preserving health and curing illnesses.

Here we find in the gift of knowledge all the requisites for almost any other gift or desire that the mind may conceive. Of course, a genie's gift of knowledge is somewhat improbable, but thus we may find out what we desire most in life. The gift of knowledge may be attained, though possibly with more difficulty than a mere wish. Knowing our ultimate desires, a primary goal in life should be a never ending search for knowledge.

LIBERTY

The terms *liberty* and *freedom* are herewith used as synonyms, with *liberty* chosen for the title because *freedom* is too closely associated with *free-will* which is discussed in FATE. Liberty is defined as a state in which all endeavors are led by reason (independent of the compulsory will of another). A mere lack of restraint or restrictions against fulfilling a desire is not freedom, for we are not free of the causes of the desire nor may we have the ability or power to fulfill our desires (e.g. one may desire and be *free* to spend a million dollars, but not have a million dollars; or desire and be *free* to run a mile in one minute, but have no legs). The power to do what one wills and to act with reason are both requisites of freedom or liberty, and there must not be an attempt to deprive others of their liberty or impede their efforts to obtain it.

A government desirous of providing liberty for its citizens would establish only those laws which compel actions that a just man would *freely* elect to do, even if the laws did not exist — only the criminal should be restrained by good laws. Man loses liberty in society when he is mistreated, misgoverned, treated unequally, or denied a voice in government when capable of ruling himself. A free man should not be degraded or used as a means by his government (e.g. sent to his death in war).

LOVE AND MARRIAGE

We speak of love of ideas, things, places, people, and God. This discourse, however, will be limited to a consideration of love as a complex emotion which should result in and become part of a lasting marriage.

In speaking of this type of love a number of questions frequently arise. Is there love at first sight? How does one distinguish between love and liking, between love and infatuation? Can a person love more than one at the same time? Can a person love more than one at any time? Before attempting to define love and answer the preceding questions it is necessary that there be an acceptance of the assumption that monogamy and marriages which result in children and last a lifetime are the best social order.

Love is frequently portrayed by having such emotional responses as the inability to eat, inability to sleep, butterflies in the stomach, and the perception of birds singing everywhere while one dreams of the object of attentions. These symptoms also are usually associated with the temporary emotion referred to as infatuation and, therefore, are not sufficient to be classified as love. Love is also frequently evaluated on the basis of degree: that is, the one I like most, want to be with most, am most compatible with is the one I love. The trouble with this type of thinking is that it is related to time and, unfortunately, at a later date it is to be expected that I may find another person whom I like still more, want to be with more, and with whom a greater degree of compatibility exists. Thus if love should lead to marriage, it is conceivable that each year a new person with successively greater attributes might be encountered and each year a new divorce and marriage would be in order.

If love should result in a lasting marriage, then judging from the present high rates of divorce, it must be concluded that a large percentage of our people are getting married without being in love. When so many do not know what love is or how to evaluate it, it is to be expected that there will be frequent marriages without love.

I will define love as being a decision. That is, a person is in love when he can make a decision to the effect that "I like this person the most, want to be with this person the most, and am more compatible with this person than any that I now know; and I shall be satisfied and do not care to wait or seek any longer for one with greater attributes, and in the interest of a lasting marriage I shall even avoid future relationships that might allow me to determine that another has greater attributes and would make a more suitable mate."

Upon the basis of defining love as a decision, there can be love at first sight; but it is thus not likely to be a wise decision. As the decision relates to one mate in a monogamous society, one cannot love more than one person at the same time. A person can have more than one love, after death has dissolved a marriage. Love is initiated only at the instant the decision is made; therefore, all relations prior to this instant can be classified no higher than liking or infatuation.

In order to make a wise decision on love, time is required for comparisons and evaluation of attributes, both virtues and shortcomings. It is more important to attempt to know all the shortcomings than all the virtues. Unexpected virtues can only reinforce the marriage; but a decision made without full recognition of the shortcomings is one that will be difficult to follow or accept.

Listed below is a group of some of the major human attributes. An evaluation of these may serve as a guide for those about to make this most important of decisions, or for those who are weighing a decision already made.

Aesthetic Taste
Ambition
Appearance
Background & Education
Chastity
Common Sense
Conversational Ability
Cooperation
Courage
Dependability
Dignity
Discretion
Flexibility
Foresight
Habits and Manners
Health
Humility
Imagination
Initiative
Interest in Children
Jealousy
Judgment

Kindness
Memory
Orderliness
Originality
Patience
Perseverance
Promptness
Recreational Interest
Religion
Reputation
Self-control
Self-Reliance
Sense of Humor
Sincerity
Social Concern
Stability
Temperance
Thrift
Tolerance
Veracity
Versatility
Vitality
Vocational Ability
Written Expression

MATURITY AND YOUTH

We often refer to young people in a derogatory fashion as being "immature." There is an inference that youth should act more wisely as do older more "mature" individuals. Whereas it is a truism that wisdom takes time to develop, and that it is more likely to be found in the older "mature" individual; it does not necessarily follow that wisdom automatically comes with aging.

There are some characteristic differences between the actions of youth and the actions of older or more "mature" individuals; and not all of those differences are in favor of the elderly. The greater idealism of youth is a characteristic which should be encouraged and not stifled as "maturity" comes. The Junior Chamber of Commerce (no official connection with the Chamber of Commerce), in recognition of the typical loss of idealism with aging, have a constitutional provision prohibiting active membership after age 35. This age limit was established to help overcome what is believed to be one of the major obstacles to organization creative endeavor. Most organizations are dominated by the respected, older leaders of the community. These older leaders have usually adjusted relatively well to whatever conditions, good or bad, that exist in a community; and they tend to prefer the status quo for fear that attempting to improve one thing may possibly upset other things which are presently quite satisfactory. When a young man proposes a significant change to an organization dominated by elders, he is typically rebuffed by such remarks as: "We can't get enough support to do it"; "Don't waste your time and ours because its been tried many times before without success"; "It can't be done"; "Leave well enough alone." The Jaycee limitation on age gives responsible young men of the community the opportunity, in their callow ignorance of the fact that "it can't be done" and of the magnitude of the obstacles they face, to use their sheer enthusiasm, "impractical" idealism, and "undignified" effort in city after city, year after year to do the things which "couldn't be done." The idealism of youth needs to be incorporated in all organizations by reserving some decision making positions for the young.

The characteristic differences in which youth measures less favorably is in their impatience, lack of self-discipline, and their tendency to seek escape (e.g. drugs, running away from home) instead of bearing the tensions long enough to solve significant problems. These relative weaknesses are to be expected because of their inexperience and confusion, their seeking to become independent of parental control, and their struggle to know themselves and establish their own value system.

One definition of the word mature is: "completely developed; fully ripe, as plants, fruit, animals, etc." This then places maturity merely as a function of age. A more satisfactory definition, as applied to humans, is: "a relative measurement of adjustment to one's environment." This latter definition is independent of age. Our educational system and our society need to work at improving the ability to adjust to one's environment, at all ages.

MEDITATION

Meditation is like the morning shower, an emotional washing or mental dusting, a removal of the clutter of the previous day and a setting in order for the day to come. It is time for peace and love and fusion with the fundamental life force. There should be a revolving, coordination and an analysis of thoughts which might include questions such as the following:

What did I do well?
What mistakes did I make?
What do I want to do today and tomorrow and how shall I do it?

What can I contribute today to the lifelong process of knowing myself and my fellow man?
What help shall I seek?
Whom shall I help?

METAPHYSICS

Early writers spoke of metaphysics as being the first philosophy or the foundation. Metaphysics is a science dealing with immaterial, intangible or non-sensible substances; while the science of physics deals with material or sensible substances. Metaphysics may be defined as the systematic study of the fundamentals relating to the ultimate nature of reality and of human knowledge. It thus falls into two divisions, namely, Ontology - the systematic study of the ultimate problems of Reality or Being, and Epistemology - the systematic study of the ultimate problems of human knowledge. Most writers use Metaphysics as being synonymous with Ontology; others make it synonymous with Epistemology.

Ontology depends essentially upon analogical inference and logical argument to deal with such topics as the existence and attributes of God, immortality, freedom of will versus fatalism, and creation. Such topics do not lend themselves to laboratory experimentation; and, therefore, some consider Ontology a pseudo-science. Yet most individuals wish to find satisfactory personal answers and beliefs related to these ultimate problems of reality; and, therefore, there is a need for Ontology.

Epistemology has been relatively neglected in the literature, and the following attempts to point out its important potential applications in the activities of the individual and society. Epistemology as the study of the ultimate problems of human knowledge is also defined by some writers as the science which deals with the presuppositions or assumptions underlying all knowledge and communication. All assumptions are presuppositions, but all presuppositions are not assumptions. A person who makes an assumption is making a presupposition about which he is aware. He is also aware that, if he were to so choose, he could make a different assumption. However, a presupposition may be made unawares, without consciousness of the possibility that others might be made instead. Every question is based upon one or more presuppositions.

If the one who asks has presuppositions which are different from the one who answers, there is no real communication. Thus if a question is asked: "Can we move this weight?" the answer might be "no" if there is a presupposition that we two have to do it manually; however, the answer would be "yes" if there is presupposition that mechanical equipment can be used. A presupposition or assumption may be true or false, or we may not know whether it is true or false. For example, when we ask for a receipt for a sum of money paid, we may do this on the presupposition that the other party is capable of being dishonest although we do not know for a fact whether or not he will be dishonest.

The proper place of Epistemology is not to decide which presuppositions are true, but to find out what presuppositions have been made in a particular instance. Much of the trouble and confusion in the world is due to unstated, unclear or differing presuppositions similar to the above example about moving a weight. The remarkable achievements in science, engineering and medicine are largely dependent upon the cooperative development of and agreement upon assumptions. Examples of cooperatively developed assumptions used in engineering are the design life of an automobile, the factor of safety to be used, and the design load on a structure. These assumptions are not developed by mathematics or equations, but usually only after elaborately considered and compromised value judgments are made at a convention. Thus one may find a code recommends (assumes) that a "safe" live load for a particular building should be 40 pounds per square foot. This does not mean that the actual live load will be 40 pounds per square foot, nor that the average or maximum load will be 40 pounds per square foot; for it is quite possible that an occupant of the building, who is completely ignorant of such things as design loads, may install equipment having a weight far exceeding the design loads. The recommended live load represents an estimate of probable maximum loads introduced by (it is hoped) intelligent users of the building. This also involves the recognition that there may possibly be unintelligent occupants; but if costs are kept within some (assumed) reasonable range, this risk must be incurred. An engineer might very justifiably argue: "I believe that human life cannot be measured in dollars. I believe that we should reduce the risk of collapse to an insignificant point, and I recommend that we should all assume design loads of 5,000 pounds per square foot." Obviously, if one engineer assumes 40 and another assumes 5000 pounds per square foot, they could never come close to agreement on how to design the building.

The relative lack of success in solving our social and political problems may largely be caused by the lack of prior agreement and cooperatively developed assumptions as has been done in science, medicine, and engineering. Most of the important intangible words used in social and political discourse such as "truth", "good", "justice", "freedom", "democracy", etc. are not clearly defined (definitions are assumptions -- see DEFINITIONS) and are ordinarily used and abused in many different ways. Disputes between nations are more likely to be resolved if there is prior agreement on such basic assumptions as the purpose of government, the rights of the individual man, the rights of individual nations, the relations between ends and means, facts and causes, applicable principles, etc. Starting out with the positive approach of establishing points of agreement on acceptable presuppositions and definitions, translated into the various languages, can be a major step in achieving solutions to our social and political problems.

NEEDS VS. WANTS

One of the major principles of Stoic philosophy is the recommendation that the path to happiness may be found by reducing one's wants. Unhappiness comes when one's wants are not realized; and if the numbers of wants are small, then there is less likelihood of disappointments in the wants going unfulfilled. The ideal to seek is to limit one's wants to necessities, and to be satisfied if one has the necessities of life.

The necessities of life might be included in the general categories of food, clothing, shelter, health care and, in many instances where public transportation is impractical; a personal means of transportation becomes a necessity. Excesses in wants related to necessities can also result in unfulfillment and unhappiness. In the instance of food, excesses could be incurred if one considered it necessary to dine every evening in the most expensive restaurants and being a host to companions in such dining. Similarly, in the instances of shelter and clothing; one could consider it necessary to own a 30 room mansion and to be continuously clothed in the latest fashion produced by the most famous designers.

Excesses come about when "more" or "better" is sought for mere vanity, or assistance and servants are enlisted when one could readily accomplish what is needed by themselves. Self-importance or success should not be measured by "lifestyle" or possessions, but by performance. How few are our real needs, how vast are our imaginary ones.

NON-LETHAL WEAPONS

The recent proliferation of guns in homes and automobiles is frequently resulting in injuries and deaths of children who find the guns, and many other injuries and deaths brought about by the combination of sudden anger and the ready availability of guns. Justification for the spreading possession of guns is the rising crime rate and the increasing concern and desire to exercise the constitutional "right of the people to bear arms." Undoubtedly, more and more people are finding police protection inadequate and feel the need to be able to protect themselves. Many face the dilemma of the desire for self-protection along with the conflicting concern about the potential for accidents or impetuous actions when guns are readily available.

A potential solution to this dilemma lies in the development and use of better non-lethal weapons. Unfortunately, the current commonly available non-lethal weapons, including mace, tear gas, tranquilizer darts, stun guns, rubber bullets, and water cannon are relatively ineffective; and their use by individuals and police is inconsequential when compared to the use of guns. However, it is believed that much more effective non-lethal weapons could be developed if a small fraction of the research and development funds used by the military establishment for lethal weapons were shifted to research and the development of better non-lethal weapons.

An inexpensive non-lethal weapon, which could in an instant and at a considerable distance temporarily incapacitate, would have a very significant effect on our social structure. Every citizen could be encouraged to have self-protection and assist in preventing crime, without fear of serious injury or death due to accidents or inappropriate use of the weapons. Police using non-lethal weapons would no longer have to worry about firing first or facing an investigation to prove that their firing a gun was justified in the particular circumstance. Criminals of all types would recognize that there is a very high probability of apprehension when almost every citizen has a weapon (assuming non-lethal weapons could be carried by each person, without need for a permit); and this high probability of apprehension will be a major deterrent to crime.

An idealistic use for non-lethal weapons could be as a substitute for lethal weapons in war. The Geneva Conference has established rules for warfare, and gas and chemical warfare have supposedly been banned. Why not establish rules which ban all lethal weapons? A ban on all lethal weapons is no more illogical than a ban on only some lethal weapons. Of course, war itself is not rational; but if we are to continue to accept war as a means of settling disputes and if we also establish rules for warfare, why not establish rules providing that wars shall be fought only with non-lethal weapons?

NON-SECTARIANISM

Most individuals profess the religions of their parents so that the choice of religion, as with the choice of original citizenship, becomes an accident of birth. Most individuals professing to be non-sectarian have made a personal reasoned choice, which was not accidental. Non-sectarianism is often confused with being irreligious, atheistic, or agnostic. More correctly, non-sectarianism is defined as not restricted to or associated with any one religion or sect. If there are a thousand different sects, at least nine hundred and ninety-nine if not all one thousand, must be wrong in one or more of their differing tenets. The informed individual professing non-sectarianism typically has noted what appears to be major deficiencies in the religious sects with which he is familiar; and he notes that there are many others who see deficiencies, for if any one sect was flawless, almost all the world would seek to belong to that one sect.

The individual choosing non-sectarianism, typically, finds no single dogma acceptable, is self-motivated, and has no need for formal or organized religion. He prefers a direct personal relationship to a higher power, or God, without having to go indirectly through institutions, rituals, and officials who tend to see themselves as sole interpreters of His/Her will. He wishes to be free to select and integrate the best parts of all religions within his personal philosophy and way of life.

NON-VIOLENT RESISTANCE

Injustice shall always exist; but in the good society, people should resist this injustice. In order to resist injustice and still maintain individual and social growth, it is necessary to find means of resistance which do not lead to violence, war, and destruction, such as non-violent resistance. Non-violence is not new among individuals — Christianity was founded upon such sayings as "Turn the other cheek"; but its application and first real understanding and success by large masses of people is relatively recent in history: Hungary 1867.

Hungary was under Austrian rule in 1867. The Hungarians were severely taxed, had no representation in the government, and for many years did not raise a significant voice to protest the heavy taxation forced upon them by the Austrians. Scattered but fruitless attempts were made to secure representation. After some time, under the leadership of some Hungarian clergyman, the people were united in their common aim of freeing themselves from the oppressive taxation; and with one voice they refused to pay the taxes. In retaliation the Austrians jailed many of the people and confiscated their lands and properties, but the Hungarians still made no attempt at a violent resistance. They stolidly waited and firmly continued their refusal to be taxed without representation. The Austrians tried to sell the confiscated lands and properties, but could find no buyers among the united Hungarian people. Attempts at transporting the movable property to Austria for sale proved to be a difficult and profitless venture. After many months of watching the government coffers gradually being depleted, the Austrians decided to grant full representation to Hungary; and thus brought about the first major victory through non-violent resistance.

More recent examples of major victories by non-violent resistance include those of Mahatmas Gandhi eliminating most of the human rights injustices imposed on the indentured workers in South Africa and on the Untouchables in India, and Martin Luther King's successes in the U.S.A. Civil Rights Movement. In order to appreciate the potential power of non-violent resistance, it is necessary to understand the psychology and principles involved.

If one man hits another and the victim strikes back, this gives the attacker reassurance and moral support. It shows that the victim's scale of moral values in regard to violence as a mode of settling differences is the same as the attacker's. A mere display of fear or anger is sufficient to have this effect; but suppose attackers meet fearless, calm, self-controlled individuals who respond to violence only by good tempered reasoning. The victims thereby state their readiness to prove their sincerity in attempting to find the truth in the dispute by means of their own suffering, instead of imposing suffering. At first the attackers are scornful and consider the victims as cowards; but an unflinching reaction displaces this attitude with curiosity and wonder, placing the attackers in a state of uncertainty. They realize that they made a mistake in thinking the opponents as cowards and are bothered by the thought that they may make another mistake about these unusual opponents, and that another mistake might be more embarrassing. If there are on-lookers the assailants lose still more poise. They begin to imagine themselves in the eyes of the on-lookers. They begin to feel their actions are a little excessive and undignified and in contrast less generous -- and even brutal. The surprising conduct presents suddenly the idea that the dispute can be settled calmly and amicably. They begin to realize that calm conduct is more dignified and more worthy of respect, and that there are values and imponderable forces even more powerful and desirable then physical force.

The non-violent resistors must have a deep conviction of the justice of their cause and have the courage to withstand anything for it. Here is true courage; it is much easier to strike back or run from one's opponents than to stand calmly while severe punishment or even death may be inflicted. They must show good humor, fairness, and kindness at all times. This can only come with a realization that all mankind is one, and fundamentally desire the same things. Righteous indignation must be replaced by constructive thinking. Every action must be open, without secrecy, and free from the slightest evasion. The aim is not to injure, crush or humiliate the opponents, but to convert and change their understanding and their sense of values so that they might join wholeheartedly with the resistors in seeking a settlement that is truly amicable and satisfying to both sides.

All military men will agree that it takes many years of training to make a good soldier. Therefore, it is logical to assume that it will also take a considerable amount of training before an individual could understand, believe, and react non-violently to injustice. Non-violence is not a cure-all, but it is a definite tool to be used and an effective alternate means of settling a dispute. It is the Utopian war of the future. A dispute can be lost by non-violent resistance; but the possibility of losing a violent dispute is just as great, if not greater. In a violent war neither side actually wins while both sides always win in a non-violent dispute. The leaders in non-violent resistance suffer the most; and, therefore, they are not as likely to invite a dispute as are violent leaders who usually sit back in safety and give orders to others to fight. Non-violence avoids the tremendous economic waste, brutality, and killing that occurs in war. The hysteria, the psychology, training, and the moral values of war tend to retard civilization and bring back the baser instincts; while nonviolent resistance is a development of the finest characteristics possible of man in the search for political, economic, and social truth.

PATRIOTISM

A common definition of patriotism is: Devotion to one's country. Another definition is: Evaluation of real estate above integrity. The disparity between these definitions raises a number of questions. Should Stephen Decatur's: "Our country, right or wrong" or Thomas Paine's: "My country is the world and my religion is to do good" be guiding principles? How does one justify the Revolutionary War or the Civil War if: "Our country, right or wrong?" If the state exists to serve the people, not people to serve the state, can geographical boundaries be more important than the individual or the family? If devotion or allegiance is to be given to a geographical boundary, should there not be a priority to that closest to the individual; that is, neighborhood, city, and state before country? It would seem to be preferable not to think of patriotism as devotion to real estate, but as devotion to principles: to harmonize practices with ideals, to elevate instruction into knowledge and knowledge into wisdom, and to provide liberty and peace.

We often tend to equate patriotism with valor and enthusiasm in war. Taxes, debts, and armies are the known instruments for bringing the many under dominion of the few. Through the army and war the discretionary power of the rulers is extended in dealing out offices, honors, and emoluments and in seducing the minds of the people. Throughout the ages people have placed a priority on the search for peace. How can we have peace as long as every country believes it has to have a standing army, as long as we recognize the institution of war as legitimate, and clothe it with the glory of patriotism?

Patriotism must be defined as devotion to principle, with the search for peace being the primary principle. Pythagoras said: "It is only necessary to make war with five things: maladies of the body, ignorance of the mind, passions of the body, sedition of the city (incitement to disorder), and discords of families."

POLITICS

There are many who believe that we should remove as much decision making as possible away from politics and politicians. It is often suggested that it would be preferable to have most decisions made by "experts" under the protection of Civil Service. However, the "experts" in our bureaucracies too often care not about courtesy or delays; they practice favoritism and negativism, and they frequently are corrupt - all of these difficult to prove. If elected officials appear to have these failings, it is not necessary to provide formal proof to remove them from power at the next election. It is better to have most decisions made by individuals who are subject to the power of the people and who may seek the advice of the "experts."

Even before the times of Plato we have sought an effective means of consistently having our most qualified in positions of leadership. The search for this means is yet going on. Perhaps someday we may find a means of measuring character, for this is the primary constituent needed in our leadership. In the interim, we must do all we can to elect the best, albeit our limitations.

The characteristics we commonly see in our politicians leave much to be desired. They rarely run for office with a cause or comprehensive plan that they call their own. Most are in the race primarily because of their own ambition, and not to perform a defined needed service. They depend on media antics or charisma to be elected. They remember the unborn have no votes; and as posterity has done nothing for them, they need not do anything for posterity. All too often, two kinds of men succeed in political life: Men of no principle, but great talent; and men of no talent, but of one principle - that of obedience to their superior.

The term politician has received a negative connotation. We need to place our candidates for elected office in two categories: politician or statesman. A politician thinks of the next election; a statesman thinks of the next generation. The statesman wishes to steer; the politician is satisfied to drift. The statesman realizes that being weak and amiable in the right, is no match for the politician tenaciously and pugnaciously in the wrong. The statesman realizes that by foregoing a part, the whole may be saved; and by yielding in a small matter, he may secure the greater. The statesman allocates part of his time to consider which laws are obsolete or need revising, instead of only adding innumerable new laws each year. The statesman realizes it takes hundreds of years to form an effective government, and too much power in a few hands controlling instruments of mass destruction can lay it in the dust in an hour.

POWER

Every desire, if it cannot be gratified instantly, brings a wish for the ability to gratify it and therefore a desire for power. There are, however, many different forms of power; and there is a very significant difference between power desired as a means and power desired as an end in itself. The individual who desires power as a means has first some other desire, such as a wish to see certain measures enacted; and then is led to seek the power to accomplish this by taking part in public affairs. The individual who desires power as an end will choose as an objective whatever program seems most likely to place him in a position of power.

No man should be trusted with power which is not balanced by the powers of other men. Excessive power almost always corrupts, and makes it easy to act hastily without due consideration of the consequences. Most significant problems do not lend themselves to urgent solutions, and the people have difficulty adapting to rapid, major changes. We generally underestimate all forms of power except that of the military and governmental force. Yet probably the greatest power of all comes from ideas and honest persuasion resulting in assent and voluntary compliance. The effects of the power of ideas and persuasion of such men as Christ, Buddha and Gandhi will through time far exceed that of any obtained by the force of the military or government. We must always seek to replace rule by violence with rule by the wisdom of those who appeal to the common desires of mankind for inward and outward peace and for an understanding of the world in which we live.

SUCCESS

Success is defined, in ordinary usage, as the obtaining of what one desires or intends. Many people bring about considerable unhappiness by having unattainable desires and then, upon the basis of the above definition, consider themselves complete failures. Other individuals manage to obtain their desires, but they find "success" to be wet ashes because the means that were used lost the respect and liking of their peers.

A better definition of success is: the achievement of progressive good - any progress whatsoever achieved by good means is success. This definition makes success readily achievable by everyone, independent of long term desires, intentions, or goals. Everyone can make some progress, however small, and thereby achieve success. Relative success may be measured by the amount and pace of progress, attained by good means.

TIME

Time has been defined as the duration measured for everything, with a beginning and an end between a past and future which reach into the realms of infinity. However, the dictionary says that duration means continuance. Continuance means permanence, and permanence is the state of being immutable. Immutable is that which resists time.

The time which we all know consists of the past, the present and the future; but the past is gone and is oblivion, the future may never be, and all we have left is the present, a minutiae, which is gone before we can say: "It is here." Where does time come from, what way does it pass, where does it go? It comes from the future, passes by the present, and goes into the past. That is, it comes from that which does not exist, passes by way of that which lacks extension, and goes into that which is no longer.

Although the above may cause some bewilderment, it should be clear to all that time is a most precious non- recoverable commodity. Most of us have approximately 70 years of 365 days to spend, which we are not usually as careful about in our spending as we are with the commodity which can be recovered, money. We would dread the thought of throwing away our life at once, but we often have no regard to throwing it away by parcels and piecemeal. We value our time highly if an employer wishes our services; but tend to hold it in low esteem if employed in our own services.

It is usually those who accomplish the least that are continually apologizing: "I couldn't find the time." Time is not found - it has to be allotted. Those who achieve a full life allot their time efficiently towards that which is truly beneficent recognizing that tomorrow cannot be assured and yesterday cannot be recalled.

TOLERANCE

A definition of tolerance is "freedom from prejudice." A definition of prejudice is: "a judgment or opinion formed before the facts are known." Unfortunately, there are an infinite number of facts. How many of this infinite number must be known before we can say we are not prejudiced? We are learning new facts every day of our lives - when have we learned enough to have formed an unprejudiced opinion? Based upon the above definition any and all of our opinions and judgments are suspect of being prejudiced. A better way of considering the concept of tolerance is:

"Allowing without active opposition." Here we must seek the golden mean between opposing nothing and opposing everything.

It has been said that the only real test of civilization is tolerance. This may infer that tolerance should be maximized; that, therefore, nothing should be opposed. A better statement is: "civilization should be measured by the ability to distinguish between what should be tolerated and what should not be tolerated." We should not tolerate injustice, ignorance, violence, waste, dictatorship, pollution, famine, epidemics, corruption, etc. We should be tolerant of matters beyond control of the individual or group (e.g., place or time of birth, race, handicaps, etc.), matters which are the results of accidents, customs and religions which do not harm others, rights of others (e.g., life, liberty and the pursuit of happiness), etc. Most important, we should encourage our differences in opinions and ways of life, as long as these are not injurious to others; for these differences are the sources of new and better ways.

TRUTH

If one were to choose a single word which was the most vital of all words to be clearly defined and understood, it should be the word truth; for it is elemental in pursuing mankind's purpose for existence. Some say truth is what you feel and see; but one may see a mirage, or railroad tracks which appear to converge in the distance. There are three very different concepts which often are incorrectly used interchangeably for the meaning of truth. These concepts are defined and discussed below:

Definitions

Reality - that which actually is, was or will be
Truth - mankind's best contemporary approximation or interpretation of a specific reality
Belief - an individual or minority group's approximation or interpretation of a specific reality

It is reasonable to assume that mankind will never know all of reality, and possibly will never have knowledge of most specific realities. For example, in order to know the specific reality of the length of an object, we would have to be able to measure its length with infinite accuracy. We can only approximate the "real" length, with the accuracy of the approximation dependent upon the sophistication of the available measuring instruments.

It is most important to understand that truth is changeable, for we are constantly improving our ability to measure and interpret and therefore make more accurate approximations of reality. The preceding definition of truth includes the word "contemporary" in order to recognize the importance of progress and the need to be willing to accept a new truth when it has been demonstrated to be a better approximation of reality. Ptolemy was able to predict the motions of the celestial bodies with considerable accuracy, based upon his theory that the Earth was a fixed sphere at the center of the universe and all the other celestial bodies rotated about the earth in perfect circles. The theory explained and predicted observed astronomical phenomena so well that the theory remained relatively unquestioned for over 1300 years. Ptolemy's geocentric theory was the best contemporary approximation - it was the truth for over 1300 years. The heliocentric theory of Copernicus, presupposing the sun to be the fixed center of the universe, explained many of the exceptions to the geocentric theory and approximated more accurately the observed phenomena - it became the new truth of its day. Similarly, as space travel became possible, Euclidean geometry and Newtonian mechanics had to be replaced by new truths.

New truths typically originate from the beliefs of an individual who has a new and different interpretation or approximation of reality. Most new beliefs are never accepted as truths because of the difficulties involved in demonstrating that they are better approximations or interpretations than the currently accepted truth. Only those beliefs which can be demonstrated to be significantly better approximations are likely to be accepted as new truths, for society is not likely to make changes for a trivial improvement. Many of the beliefs which became new truths were initially considered "crackpot" or "heretic." We should encourage those with new and different beliefs to demonstrate that their beliefs are significantly better, as long as the demonstrations do not involve violence.

There is not enough time in a lifetime to know all truths. Having a limited capacity we face the decision as to what truths we should seek to know, and also a means of discriminating is needed if the assumption can be made that all truths are not of equal importance. We should be most concerned with those truths which have the greatest generality, particularly those involving the individual and social existence of man. Ordinarily, we would be less concerned with determining random, uncorrelated truths such as counting the number of blades of grass in a specific square foot of the front lawn or counting the number of grains of sand in a cubic foot of earth underneath the grass, than we would be in determining the general characteristics of all blades of grass or all grains of sand. The correlation between several truths is also more important than the finding of an isolated truth.

TYRANNY-TOTALITARIANISM

If any point in political theory is indisputable it would seem to be that tyranny (cruel and unjust use of power) is the worst corruption of government. Yet we see tyranny all too prevalent, even in modern times (e.g., Hitler, Mussolini, Stalin, Mao, Castro). These modern tyrannical governments were generally started in the guise of democracy, and understanding their origins and methods of functioning may help avoid tyranny in the future.

The tyranny of totalitarianism differs from older forms of dictatorship by having a staged approval or acclamation of the acts of a Leader, or a monopoly of a single political party claiming to represent the general will of the people. Techniques used for domination include: denial of the right of existence of competing parties, abolition of personal liberty, and a closed compulsory system defined in terms of an ideological sense of mission for a greater nation - rejecting certain aspects of the past, along with glowing claims about the future. There are also, typically, attributes of infallibility, a pseudo religious worship by the masses, a dogma of consensus, and full control of the means of communication and of the economy and social relations. There is a pseudo democratic fiction that by manipulated plebiscites, mass meetings, and other emotional processes of communication the people are directly linked to and represented by the Leader.

There is a future danger of tyranny becoming established whenever social crises, emotional need for security, ideological conviction, and the hunger for power coincides. There may follow a general belief that the severe problems can only be solved by concentrating all forces in one power agency and by subduing individual freedom in exchange for sensational promises by a deified Leader. This danger becomes greater as the size of the bureaucracy in a democratic government increases, for the mass of bureaucrats can readily be made to show allegiance to the Leader. To avoid tyranny the ideals of democracy (see DEMOCRACY) must be strongly entrenched in the people: possessions of the supreme power should be by the body of the people, the rights of the individual is more important than the rights of the state, and the people must not become over dependent upon their leaders.

UNCERTAINTY AND DESPAIR

There come times to us all when the uncertainty of the future and the fear that our efforts may be wasted cause us to refrain from attempting to achieve our desires. Thus, wanting to own and live in a single-family home we exist temporarily in an apartment, because we fear the greater responsibilities of a single-family home or that we may be moving to another city shortly. Within this apartment we do nothing to improve our condition because after all it is only a temporary substitute (a temporary substitute for that which may never be - and what is there in life that is not temporary?). We desire many things, but we wait. We wait till the war is over. We wait till we are feeling better. We wait till the holiday is over. We wait until we have a holiday. We wait till the cold of winter has passed. We wait until the heat of summer has passed. We wait till we get a better salary. Waiting, always waiting, postponing, and destroying the essence of life. We shall always be able to visualize a better time than now to do our task; and when even that better time comes we will have before us something still better, and therefore may always be waiting.

Suppose that we start on some great undertaking and circumstances causes us to fail, in this case our labors were in vain; but had we never started, failure was certain regardless of circumstances. In not taking the initiative we would have lost that much of life, lost the happy prospects of success. The realization of doing things, of possible accomplishment, of knowledge gained, more than compensates for most losses accompanying failure.

No matter how uncertain are the immediate prospects, we must start now. Some efforts will fail; but having tried many times, we shall succeed many times. He who tries only those few times when favorable conditions exist, at best can only succeed a few times. If we lose material things in our failing, these material things gained once can be gained again; and having our previous knowledge we can gain them again with greater rapidity and less effort. The wise man realizes that only he who makes no effort is exempt from failure. The greatest perfection is not in never falling, but in rising every time we fall.

If tomorrow were to be your last day on this earth, how would you spend the day? Probably doing all those important things that had been neglected or postponed, living life out to its fullest. So should each day be spent, living life to the utmost of ones capability, living each day realizing that tomorrow may not come.

UTOPIA

The word "Utopia" derives from two Greek words meaning "good place" and "no place" — the "no place" generally infers it does not exist, but is only imaginary. A dictionary definition of the adjective "utopian" is: excellent, but existing only in fancy or theory. The word "Utopia" first occurred in Sir Thomas Moore's *Utopia*, published in 1516, describing a society which he considered an earthly paradise. A multitude of other authors, starting with

Hesiod (circa 750 B.C.), have added their descriptions of an ideal society to the world's literature. None of these "Utopias" has received any wide acceptance as an ideal to be worked toward; hence, a dictionary definition of the noun "utopia" is: a visionary, impractical scheme for social improvement. Most of the Utopias described in the literature fail to recognize the obvious defects in human nature. Looking back at the specifics of the societies described in earlier Utopias, they do not seem feasible in today's world, even if the proposals had plausible elements at the time of writing. It is unlikely that anyone will ever be able to develop the specifics of an ideal society which could stand unchanged for the use of many future generations.

Even if we could achieve the perfect society today, would we necessarily want to live in such a society? Would we want to live in a perfect world where there is nothing to improve, no progress to be made, nothing to look forward to, and where the differences between pleasure and pain and joy and sorrow are unknown? If not, then the concept of Utopia must be a society which is not perfect, but which is continually making significant improvements and progress toward defined ideal goals. Whereas we may never have a perfect functioning society, we can have a Utopia if it is defined as a society which has ideal practical goals toward which it is continually and effectively striving.

Thus, we can have Utopia today if we could obtain general agreement on what the important positive goals of society should be; and there is agreement to continually review these goals for needed changes or additions as the functioning of our society advances. It is possible now to establish ideal practical goals for society which could stand unchanged for many, many future generations. The following are examples of possible ideal goals for "Utopia":

1. To correct immediately any infringements upon human rights, particularly the inalienable rights of the Declaration of Independence: life, liberty and the pursuit of happiness.
2. To strive to eliminate the common plagues of mankind: poverty, disease, ignorance and injustice.
3. To establish the paramount priorities of subject matter and allocations of time needed for formal education.
4. To seek forms of government where the body of the people possess the supreme power, where a large percentage of the people are directly involved in governmental processes, and where the individuals do not become over dependent upon their leaders.
5. To encourage diversity of cultures and governments so that all may benefit by imitating the individual group's new and better ideas and learning from their mistakes.

6. To seek to resolve all disputes by non-violent means such as mediation, arbitration and the courts.

VOLUNTEERISM

Many of our public services were provided by volunteers in earlier days in the U.S.A. Volunteer fire departments were common, many public officials such as Mayors and Councilman served without pay, and many other public services were administered by Boards and Commissions which served without pay. One largely overlooked reason for this country's special feeling about the John F. Kennedy era is that he brought back some of the previous spirit of volunteerism via the Peace Corp, VISTA and the National Teacher Corps.

Today we see elected officials and civil servants seeking pay and pensions that are equal to or higher than that of the private sector, and they feel that they must operate out of palatial quarters aided by multiple assistants each of which also are to be paid at rates equal to or higher than the private sector. Each of society's problems ostensibly needs a governmental bureaucracy to attempt a solution, with ever increasing demands for more taxes to fund their activities. However, it should be becoming clear that tax supported bureaucracies are not going to be able to generate enough funds to provide the police to keep neighborhoods safe, the teachers needed to provide excellent schools, the medical personnel to maintain the health of our nation, the assistance needed by the poor and the homeless, etc. -- more individuals need to become involved in providing public services, far more than can be supported by taxes.

Our society is becoming ever more dependent upon the service industries and services provided by governmental agencies. We can provide needed services, at no direct cost, to those who cannot afford to pay for the services by an extended use of volunteerism; and by recreating the idealism needed to attract competent and energetic individuals who would place the honor of serving the public above material rewards. Voluntary service affords an unusual self-satisfaction largely because one fulfills a self-chosen purpose, instead of a purpose assigned by others.

Deferred material awards might be forthcoming from private sector positions obtained after developing a reputation in public service, as a volunteer.

A suggested ideal future government might be one in which all elected officials are part-time and unpaid, with an adequate corps of volunteer unpaid assistants. Civil Service would be operated by a very small core of full-time personnel, willing to serve as a privilege and honor with relatively low pay and pensions. The full-time Civil Service personnel would supervise a very large percentage of the needed personal who are part-time unpaid volunteers. Whereas the efficiency of equal working hours of part-time personnel is less than full-time personnel, the total number of part-time volunteer hours that could be available would far exceed the total number of full-time working hours that could be supported by taxes under today's working environment; and, therefore, the total productivity of the volunteers would be far greater.

Primary sources of volunteers could be students during after school hours, weekends and summer vacations (such public service might well reduce the attraction to drugs, gangs, etc.) and retirees most of whom would appreciate and enjoy the opportunity to serve, particularly if transportation, lunch, and protection against civil liability was provided. Idealism could be extended so that most individuals working 40 hours or less per week would find that society expected them to serve as a volunteer for a few hours per week either in public service or for non-profit organizations. An additional incentive might be an income tax deduction for volunteers, which could result in operational costs savings far in excess of the loss of tax revenue. An additional source of volunteers might be non-violent criminals who could be assigned volunteer work hours, beyond what might be expected of ordinary citizens, sufficient to compensate for the cost of their crimes and thus also eliminating the cost of keeping them in prison where they are also likely to become embittered and trained for a higher level of crime upon release.

WORLD GOVERNMENT-WORLD PEACE

Many individuals have had the opinion that we shall never have world peace until we have world government. If this opinion is correct, world peace will be long in coming for there is little or no impetus for world government that is evident today. The League of Nations and the United Nations were established as attempts at achieving world peace, without world government. World War II and the almost continuous "small" wars appear to make it obvious that their approach to achieving world peace has little or no chance to succeed without some drastic changes.

The failures of the League of Nations and the United Nations does not necessarily mean that we should discard any attempts at cooperation between free and independent nations, and that the only hope for world peace is to work for a world government. A world government, because of its massive size and complexity, is very likely to be inefficient, out of touch with the people, and have laws which are unjust to many, many individuals. Having the world government, by definition, may eliminate wars between nations as there would only be one nation. However, instead of wars between nations, we would probably have continuous violent revolutions against fumbling, incompetent world government. It is believed that the failures of the League of Nations and the United Nations lie in the founding principles being inadequate; and that cooperation between nations can result in the eventual elimination of war and revolution, if certain key principles are the foundations of such cooperation.

Wars and revolutions, in recent history, have generally come about as resistance to dictatorship, the result of discrimination against minorities, attempts to take unfair economic advantages, attempts to right past "wrongs," etc. These "reasons" for war and/or revolution can typically be placed in the single category of "infringements upon human rights." If infringements upon human rights are the primary causes of wars and revolutions, it is reasonable to assume that cooperation between nations founded upon the key principle of the preservation of human rights may succeed in eliminating wars and revolutions. The founding principles must indicate that human rights are inalienable, or God given, and that no man or government may under any circumstances take away an individual's life, liberty (including free elections), or the pursuit of happiness (including property, without due compensation). Before this could be a successful founding principle the various societies and educational systems must provide a true understanding and acceptance of the implications of human rights being inalienable, and movement is needed to remove capital punishment (see CAPITAL PUNISHMENT) as evidence of the understanding and acceptance of the concept of inalienable.

Today's nations are so interdependent that ostracizing and economic sanctions by all other nations would generally force changes in any government which clearly was infringing upon human rights. Cooperation between nations thus should also have as a founding principle that all will apply sanctions when a well-grounded complaint, followed by an unbiased inspection, results in an adjudication that human rights are being violated. The founding principles must also include an agreement by all nations to permit unbiased inspections, based upon well-grounded complaints about specific functions such as election procedures and operation of courts and penal systems. If infringements upon human rights are the primary causes of wars and revolutions, then halting these violations at an early stage provides hope for world peace.

www.ingramcontent.com/pod-product-compliance
Lightning Source LLC
Chambersburg PA
CBHW030119010526
44116CB00005B/316